365 Things
Every New Mom
Should Know

Linda Danis

HARVEST HOUSE PUBLISHERS

EUGENE, OREGON

Cover by e210, Eagan, Minnesota

Cover photos © Shutterstock; iStockphoto

Parents, please note: You are advised to consult with your pediatrician or other medical practitioner before implementing the suggestions that follow. Neither the author nor the publisher assumes any liability for possible adverse consequences as a result of the information contained herein.

365 THINGS EVERY NEW MOM SHOULD KNOW

Copyright © 2002 by Linda Danis
Published by Harvest House Publishers
Eugene, Oregon 97402
www.harvesthousepublishers.com

ISBN 978-0-7369-2382-8 (pbk.)
ISBN 978-0-7369-4726-8 (eBook)
The Library of Congress has cataloged the edition as follows:

Library of Congress Cataloging-in-Publication Data
   Danis, Linda, 1962–
      365 things every new mom should know / Linda Danis.
         p. cm.
      ISBN 978-0-7369-0923-5
      1. Motherhood.   2. Mother and child.   3. Child rearing.   I. Title: Three hundred sixty five things every new mom should know.   II. Title.

HQ759.D2635 2002

396.874'3—dc21   2001051583

Printed in the United States of America

12 13 14 15 16 17 18 19 / BP-CF / 10 9 8 7 6 5 4 3 2 1

To my husband, Dave,
and my children, Lisa, J.J., Brian, and Kevin.
You are my greatest joy and my greatest treasure!

Acknowledgments

To my children, Lisa, J.J., Brian, and Kevin: God has blessed me with the four best children a mother could ever hope for. You are truly His most special gifts to me.

To my husband, Dave: This book never could have been written without your help, support, and encouragement. You are the best! I love you.

To my parents, Barbara and Charlie Reynolds: Thank you for the solid foundation you gave me in a secure and loving home. Thanks also for being such devoted grandparents.

To Melinda Blake, Claire Humphrey, Steve Kay, and Jenny Lyons: Thank you for reading through this manuscript and offering me feedback, input, and encouragement.

To all my mom friends whom I have met through playgroups, school, church, and the neighborhood: I have learned something from each of you as we have come alongside each other on this journey of motherhood.

To Kim Moore: Thank you for your valuable editing skills, insight, and encouragement. It was a delight to work with you.

To Bob Hawkins, Sr., Carolyn McCready, LaRae Weikert, Barb Sherrill, Betty Fletcher, and all the others at Harvest House: Thank you for believing in this book and making it a reality.

To my Lord and Savior, Jesus Christ: Thank You for giving me the wisdom, strength, and patience to help me be the mother You want me to be. Please take this book and use it for Your glory!

Contents

∞

The Fourth Three Months ~ A Bundle of Energy
199

Determining Your Priorities ∽ Living in Contentment ∽
The Moral Training of Our Children ∽ Spending Time in
God's Word ∽ Lead by Your Example ∽ Enjoy Your Child's
World ∽ The Need to Discipline ∽ Learning to Be a Better
Mom ∽ Grow in Your Relationship with the Lord ∽
Brothers and Sisters ∽ How to Discipline Your Child ∽ Use
Your Time Wisely ∽ Our Children Change Us
for the Better

May the Lord Bless You
267

Mother to Mother

Congratulations on your new baby. I am so excited for you! You probably feel a mixture of awe, anxiety, and excitement for this little person, this miracle, this gift given to you by God. What a special time of life you are entering!

In the pages ahead you will find encouragement, practical tips, and spiritual insight on a daily basis to help you become the mother you always hoped to be. This book is filled with the nuts and bolts of parenting. Games, songs, activities, and advice will help you nurture your baby's physical, social, intellectual, and emotional development as well as encourage your child's spiritual and moral growth. All of these interactive activities are easy to do and require only a few minutes of time.

At the end of each week there is a devotion that will nurture you as a mom. So many changes are happening in your life right now that it can be a bit overwhelming. These reflections will help guide you down the path of motherhood, giving you perspective, encouragement, and godly counsel. They will help you grow in your faith as you depend more on God to meet the new challenges of parenting. And they will point you toward God as the source of all patience, strength, and wisdom.

I began writing this book when my fourth child was born so I would know exactly what a new mother was experiencing and would need to know. I pray that it will give you the confidence and skills necessary to become an effective, godly mother who enjoys and cherishes her new role.

This book isn't meant to be read all at once, but instead should be used as a daily companion to guide you through your baby's first year, one day at a time. You might find it handy to keep it on your nightstand or by the changing table. My goal is to make sure you have just the information you need when you need it. It's my hope that reading this book will be like receiving a daily phone call from a good friend who can offer you advice and helpful insight gleaned from twelve years experience as a mother of four.

Whether this is your first child, and you don't know what to expect, or your fourth child, and you're too busy to read up on what you should be doing and need some fresh ideas, you will benefit from *365 Things Every New Mom Should Know*. The first year of a baby's life is an exciting time of new discoveries, phenomenal brain growth, and the beginning of an intense love affair between mother and child. This book will help you lay a foundation of love, trust, and closeness for your baby that will last a lifetime.

Warmly,
Linda Danis

The First
Three Months

A Bundle of Joy

My child, you hold the whole of
my heart in your small hands.

AUTHOR UNKNOWN

Week 1

Day 1

After all these long months, your precious little baby has finally arrived. The child you have longed for is here to hold, to look at, and to touch. Your baby will look up at you and recognize your familiar voices. You are the ones he has been longing to meet—his mommy and daddy! Get to know your sweet little baby—hold him, rock him, smell his skin, gaze at him, marvel at his tiny fists, caress him. Treasure this awesome miracle!

Day 2

On the day you bring your baby home for the first time, have everyone in your family place their hands on her and pray for her. This will be a precious moment for your family to share together as you welcome her into your family and give thanks to God for this wonderful gift!

Day 3

If you have older children who want to hold their new sibling, use a nursing "donut pillow" to help them support your baby's head. Have your child sit all the way back on the couch. Place the semicircle nursing pillow around his waist. Set your baby on the pillow with his bottom wedged in between your older child's tummy and the pillow. Rest your baby's head on your older child's arm that is resting on the pillow. Even if your child lets go of the baby, his head will still be secure on the pillow. Of course, you should always be sitting right next to your new baby, monitoring his safety. This also works for young visitors, but I would suggest waiting a week or two before letting a nonfamily-member child hold your baby.

Day 4

Despite what all the books may say, most women experience some soreness (or a lot of soreness!) in the first weeks of nursing. Try using your Lamaze breathing when your baby latches onto your breast. If your nipples are cracked or blistered, blot them dry with a cotton diaper after you have finished nursing. Saliva has enzymes that can irritate sore nipples. After you have dried the saliva off, express a little milk and rub it on your nipples. Let them air dry. Also, do not look down at your baby the entire time you nurse. This position can strain your neck and cause tension headaches. If you can persevere through the first two weeks of nursing, things will get better.

Day 5

Sometimes as a new parent it's hard to tell whether or not you should call your pediatrician. If you are reluctant to call your doctor in the middle of the night, you can usually call the nursery at the hospital where you gave birth. The nurses are awake and can advise you as to whether you should call your doctor right away or if it can wait until the morning. Do *not* wait if your baby has a fever higher than 99.9 degrees rectally (this is the most accurate way to take your baby's temperature). Call your doctor immediately.

Day 6

Drink water every time you nurse to stay hydrated and to maintain your milk supply. Always keep a water bottle close at hand. It is a good idea to set up a "nursing station" wherever you will be nursing the most. Have everything you need right at hand—a water bottle, a burp cloth, a nursing pillow, a book or magazine to read, and nursing pads.

Day 7

When your baby startles while lying on her back (the Moro reflex), gently but firmly hold her hands together close to her chest to calm her and make her feel more secure. Say, "It's okay, sweetheart. Mommy will help you." This reflex will disappear by four months.

Reflections on the Week

I prayed for this child, and the LORD has granted me what I asked of him.

1 SAMUEL 1:27

Before I formed you in the womb I knew
you, before you were born I set you apart.

JEREMIAH 1:5

An Incredible Love

You have had your baby only one short week and yet you can hardly remember what life was like without him. You prepared for months for his arrival—read books, set up the nursery, went to prenatal classes—yet nothing could prepare you for the overwhelming love you feel for this child. There are no words quite powerful enough to describe the emotions you feel.

Then the impossible happened; each day you grew to love him more. The sheer magnitude of love takes your breath away. Can there be anything more wonderful than when he gazes into your eyes, when you feel his small body curled up in your arms, when you feel his warm breath on your cheek, when his little fingers wrap tightly around yours? Your heart is ready to burst with this new miracle in your life.

It doesn't matter if this is your first or fifth child, the profound love you feel for your new baby never changes. I remember during my second pregnancy, I secretly worried that I might not love this new baby as much as my first. How could I ever love another child as much as I loved her? But the moment I held my new baby, I knew immediately I had worried for nothing. There was no difference in my love. It was as amazingly wonderful and intense as the love I had for my first. It happened again when my third and fourth children were born. We don't have to divide our love between our children. Our love actually multiplies, giving us even more love to share. It is one of the ways God's love works in motherhood. We just have more and more love to give away!

Dear God, thank You for this precious little baby. He is everything I prayed for. Everything about him is perfect. Words can hardly describe how much I love him. Because of him, I have a better idea now of how much You, my heavenly Father, love me. Please help me adjust to all the changes I will face as a new mother. Amen.

Week 2

Day 8

Try to take at least one nap a day to maintain your energy level. You need your rest too! As you know, a tired, grumpy mother is of no use to anyone. This is especially true if you are nursing, because it will help your body be able to keep up your milk supply in the evening hours.

Day 9

When your baby is fussy, try holding him on your left side close to your heart. He will be comforted by the sound of your heartbeat. Swaddle him in a blanket to make him feel secure. Use a gentle voice and soft caresses. Remember, all the sounds, lights, and tastes are new to him and can be a bit overwhelming at times.

Day 10

Don't worry about making your baby's room dark or having everyone in the house be completely quiet while she sleeps. It is better for her to get used to sleeping through some noise and light from the very beginning.

Day 11

Help your baby get his days and nights straight by not letting him sleep more than three to four hours between feedings during the day. Wake him up to feed him. The old adage "don't wake a sleeping baby" doesn't hold true here. You want to help his body get in the rhythm of taking naps during the day and sleeping long stretches during the night. If you're nursing, this will also help you establish a good milk supply in the first weeks.

Day 12

Remember that the telephone is there for your convenience. If you are busy feeding your baby, changing a diaper, or just enjoying snuggling with her, let the answering machine get the call. You do not always have to drop everything to answer the phone. Return the call at a more convenient time.

Day 13

Encourage your husband to help take care of your baby from the beginning so he will gain confidence in handling her. If you give too many corrections, he may just relinquish all childcare duties to you, "the expert." He may do things differently than you, but that's okay.

It's time for your baby's
two-week checkup.

Day 14

Be prepared for your baby's doctor appointments. Write down any questions you may have so you don't forget anything. Purchase a small medical notebook to keep track of doctor visits (things discussed, measurements), illnesses (symptoms, duration), injuries, vaccinations, medicines (any reactions), treatments, and allergies. This will be helpful when you need to fill out school forms, to note patterns of reoccurring problems, to remember medicines that have been taken, or if you have to switch doctors.

Reflections on the Week

Children are a heritage from the LORD, the fruit of the womb is a reward. Like arrows in the hand of a warrior, so are the children of one's youth. Happy is the man who has his quiver full of them.

PSALM 127:3-5 NKJV

With man this is impossible, but not with God: all things are possible with God.

MARK 10:27

Children Are Gifts

Children are gifts from God to love, cherish, nurture, and enjoy. A miracle has been bestowed upon you. Your child will touch your heart in ways you cannot predict. Motherhood is such a privilege and blessing. You probably cried with joy when you first held her warm, tiny body in your arms. God has created her to be absolutely unique, and you can be sure He has a special plan for her. What an awesome responsibility you have! God chose you to be this child's mother because nobody else would do. Right now, you are the most important person in your baby's life.

Babies are completely helpless and depend on us for every need. Being a mother can be both exhilarating yet difficult, fulfilling yet exhausting. At times it can feel downright overwhelming. You may wonder, "How can I possibly take care of my baby? I have never done this before." The good news is you are not alone. God created motherhood! He knows everything there is to know about it—the frustrations, the limitations, and the joys. You can trust that God will help you raise this child He has entrusted to your care. He has promised to help if you will go to Him and ask.

*D*ear *Heavenly Father, I love this child, this gift You have given to me, more than words can say. I so much want to be a good mother. Please fill me with Your wisdom, Your gentleness, and Your patience as I enter this new role as a mother. Guide me day-by-day, hour-by-hour. Thank You, Lord. Amen.*

Week 3

Day 15

Try to keep your baby awake during feedings, otherwise he will get used to snacking instead of receiving a full feeding. Work on getting him to nurse at least five minutes on each side, preferably ten. To wake him up, try changing his diaper, rubbing his feet, or sitting him up. Remember to burp him after nursing on each side; otherwise the air bubble might make him feel full and cause him to stop nursing, even though he didn't take in much milk.

Day 16

Your baby is ready for a real bath once her umbilical cord has fallen off. Gather everything you will need and place it within close reach. Keep a firm, protective hand on her and speak soothingly. If she seems fearful, just go back to giving her a sponge bath for a while. Wait a week or two and then try giving her a tub bath again.

Day 17

Help your baby get his day into a predictable routine where he eats first, then is awake for a while, and then takes a nap. Once he becomes used to this pattern, there will not be as much crying because he knows he will be fed soon after he wakes up, when he is hungry. He will be awake when his tummy is full, so he is happy. He will be put to bed when he is beginning to get tired, but before he gets cranky. You will find that his time awake with you will be more enjoyable because he is well rested, full, and happy.

Day 18

Don't wait until your child is older before you start praying with her. Pray out loud with her every night before she goes to sleep. A simple, short prayer is best. One prayer might be, "Thank You, Jesus, for this day. Please bless Mommy, Daddy, and _____. Please let us have love in our hearts. Amen."

Day 19

When you dispose of a dirty diaper, roll it up tightly and then fasten the bundle together with the tabs. This helps the diaper take up less room in the diaper pail and helps hold in the smell. It also keeps the adhesive tabs from sticking to the trash bag and tearing it when you try to pick up the bag.

Day 20

Cutting your baby's tiny fingernails can be difficult, but if you don't she will tend to scratch her face. It is easiest to do when she is asleep in her car seat so she is not moving around. Pull the skin away from the nail so there will be less chance of cutting her. You can use nail clippers, baby scissors, or an emery board.

Day 21

Often friends will lend you baby clothes and equipment. Keep a list of what has been borrowed so you can remember what needs to be returned after it is outgrown. When you receive new clothes for your baby, wash them right away to allow for shrinkage. Clothing you thought wouldn't fit for months may fit right now!

Reflections on the Week

He gives strength to the weary and increases the power of the weak...but those who hope in the LORD will renew their strength. They will soar on wings like eagles; they will run and not grow weary, they will walk and not be faint.

ISAIAH 40:29-31

May the LORD answer you when you are in distress...May he send you help...May he remember all your sacrifices...May he

*give you the desires of your heart and
make all your plans succeed.*

PSALM 20:1-4

The Postpartum Blues

As your body is recovering from pregnancy and child-birth, there are many physical and hormonal changes taking place. You may feel weepy, overwhelmed, and discouraged. In addition, anyone who came to help has probably left, leaving you to feel all alone. It is okay to feel nervous and overwhelmed at first, but you don't need to stay in this state of despair and discouragement. You have a loving God who promises to give you strength. He is never too busy or distracted to hear your cries for help. Many women experience "the blues" and are able to bounce back on their own. For a few others, the depression is more serious and long lasting. If you are not feeling better in a couple weeks, contact your physician. There may be a medical condition that is causing your depression.

You are never alone in your responsibilities as a mother. God is always there through all your problems and challenges. He is present during bouts of colic, middle-of-the-night feedings, messy diapers that require a change of clothes *and* bedding, and the spit up that lands all over the carpet. You don't need to carry all the burdens of the day by yourself. Instead, give them over to the Lord and depend on Him. He is there to help even in the little things of life.

Of course, you also need to do your part—get plenty of rest by taking naps, eat nutritious food, and drink plenty of water. Give yourself credit for all you are accomplishing on only a few hours of sleep a night. Caring for a baby takes an incredible amount of time; everything takes longer than expected. Begin by lowering your expectations as to what you can get done, and then just take one day at a time. It really does get easier. You will survive all the challenges of parenting. You are going to be a great mom!

Dear Father, I'm feeling a little overwhelmed right now and very tired. As much as I love my baby, some days are so difficult. Lord, I place my hope in You. Please give me strength to not just get through each day, but to enjoy and cherish each one. Help me to take care of myself so I can in turn take care of this bundle of joy You have given me. Help me be a patient, tender mother. Thank You for never being too busy to hear my prayers. Amen.

Week 4

Day 22

A pacifier can be a real lifesaver. It can help calm your baby and allow him to satisfy his additional sucking needs when he is not hungry. If your baby uses a pacifier, have several on hand. Designate one or two spots (for example, the corner of the crib) to keep them so they do not get lost around the house. Whenever you come across one lying around, rinse it off and then put it back in the designated spot. Now you won't be caught empty-handed the next time you need one!

Day 23

Even though you are probably exhausted, try to relax and enjoy the middle-of-the-night feedings with your baby. These quiet moments alone can be special, and even more so if you have other children around during the day. Take comfort in knowing you are not the only person up in the wee hours of the morning. Think of all the other mothers who are also awake feeding their babies at that very moment.

Day 24

It's not too early to start that age-old tradition—the wall growth chart. Find a door or wall and make your first marks with your baby's height at birth and from her first checkup. It will be fun to look back over the years to see how much she has grown.

Day 25

Take your baby on a house tour. Hold him facing out and point to things around the house. Talk about what happens in each of the rooms. He will enjoy seeing all the new sights, being walked around, and hearing your voice.

Day 26

When loading your diaper bag, remember to put in a change of clothes for your baby in case of spit up or a leaky diaper. Also keep some resealable plastic bags on hand for soiled diapers.

Day 27

Your baby's hair will probably change color in the next year. To help you remember what that downy newborn hair looked like, trim some off the back of her head by the nape of her neck. It's an inconspicuous spot, and you will cherish that lock of baby hair in the years to come.

Day 28

Sing often to your baby. Any song will do. She will love to hear the rhythm of your voice. Try "Twinkle, Twinkle, Little Star."

Twinkle, twinkle, little star, how I wonder what you are

Up above the world so high, like a diamond in the sky

Twinkle, twinkle, little star, how I wonder what you are

Reflections on the Week

He who began a good work in you will carry it on to completion until the day of Christ Jesus.

PHILIPPIANS 1:6

Above all, love each other deeply, because love covers a multitude of sins.

1 PETER 4:8

The Perfect Mother

Did you enter into parenthood as I did, wanting to be the "perfect" mother? You are only a few weeks into this, and already you may be falling short of the ideal of perfection you had in mind before you had children. Relax. It's okay, because perfection isn't a requirement for parenting! Life simply can't be lived without making some mistakes. Your baby doesn't realize you are inexperienced. He has no one to compare you to. In your baby's trusting eyes, you are perfect! He loves you just the way you are.

In your quest to be a good mom, you have two important things on your side. First, you are in this with a perfect God who is always available to give you strength and wisdom. Second, He has already given you the most important thing you need—an unconditional love for your child. This love covers many mistakes. Everything else you can learn to do, but the unconditional love you feel for your child is a gift from God. It is a love that is patterned after God's own love for you. This love will help carry you through all the trials and tribulations of parenting.

Dear God, thank You so much for this child You have given me. I so much want to be the best possible mother for my baby. Help me to know what to do so I can be

the mother You want me to be. I feel such an incredible love for my child that I would do anything for him. Thank You for unconditionally loving me. Thank You that Your love doesn't depend on how good I am, but instead it stems from who You are. Amen.

Week 5

Day 29

To help keep track of all those "firsts" and memorable moments, jot them down on your calendar as they happen. Later, when you have the time, it will be easier to fill in your child's baby book.

Day 30

The thing your baby likes to look at the most, more than anything else, is your face. Hold him close when you cuddle or rock him. Look in his eyes, smile, and use his name often to show him how important he is to you. Give him your undivided attention. Your loving touches are just as important to his health as taking care of his nutritional needs.

Day 31

Let Jesus' name be one of the first words your baby hears. As you take care of her say, "God made you, _____, and I am so glad He did," or "Mommy loves _____ and so does Jesus." Your baby will begin to associate Jesus' name with gentle touches and comforting words.

Your Baby Is One Month Old!

Day 32

Turn on some slow music or simply hum as you hold your baby close and gently dance to the music. Enjoy the special relationship that is deepening between the two of you!

Day 33

You can begin to work on getting your legs toned again while you entertain your baby. Place your baby on a blanket on the floor, next to the couch. Stand with your feet together and lean your hands on the arm of the couch. Lift your leg behind you twelve times while maintaining eye contact with your baby. Repeat with the other leg. Next lift your leg to the side twelve times on each leg. Do this whenever you have a chance during the day.

Day 34

When your baby is on her tummy and can't see you, put your cheek next to hers, rub her back, and talk tenderly to her. She will learn that even when she can't see you, you are there for her—just like our heavenly Father.

Day 35

You will be spending a lot of time changing your baby's diapers. You can either see this as drudgery or as an opportunity to talk to him, play with him, sing to him, and do many of the activities that are presented in this book. Even the most mundane tasks can be made more enjoyable when you look at them from a new perspective!

Reflections on the Week

For God so loved the world that he gave his one and only Son, that whoever would believe in him shall not perish but have eternal life.

JOHN 3:16

For it is by grace you have been saved, through faith—and this not from yourselves, it is the gift of God—not by works, so that no one can boast.

EPHESIANS 2:8-9

A Relationship with God

As you have read through the devotions each week, does all this talk about God make you feel a little uncomfortable or seem a little trite? Perhaps talking about God as someone you know personally, and who is there to help you daily, is a new concept or maybe a long forgotten one from your past. For most people, having a baby is a time when we step back to reconsider what we believe and what our spiritual framework is as a family. Becoming a parent often renews or deepens our faith. Certainly, experiencing the miracle of childbirth reveals to us the goodness and existence of God.

God isn't distant. He isn't a magic genie or someone to think about just at Christmas and Easter. He is real and personal and is interested in your life. He loves you and created you to be in a close, intimate relationship with Him—a friendship closer than any other. He desires to have that relationship with you, but it's your choice whether you respond to His offer. To enter into a relationship with Him, you must simply admit that you need Him.

God is holy and perfect, yet as humans we have all fallen short of that perfection and have sinned. They might be big, obvious sins or hidden sins that no one else knows about except God. God sent His Son to bridge the gap between His holiness and our sin. Jesus died on the cross as a payment for all our past, present, and future sins so we could be forgiven, have a relationship with Him here on earth, and then live with Him forever in heaven. When we believe this and desire for God to be in our lives, He will come. Everything won't be perfect, but

He will walk with us and give us the strength, direction, comfort, and wisdom to be the kind of mothers, wives, and women He wants us to be.

Dear God, I believe in You, but I want to know You better. I want to walk closer to You and not try to live life on my own. I want my ways to be Your ways. Please forgive me for all my thoughts, attitudes, and actions that have been wrong. Thank You that You sent Your Son to pay the ransom for my sins. I accept Your gift of salvation through Jesus Christ. Please come be a part of my life, especially now as I embark on this wonderful journey of motherhood. Amen.

Week 6

Day 36

When your baby is fussy, pray with her so she can hear you go to God in times of trouble. You might say, "Jesus, please comfort _____," or "Dear Jesus, help _____ to feel better."

Day 37

Make a permanent baby-sitter information card on a 5 x 7 index card. List your name, address, and phone number (to be able to give to a dispatcher in an emergency). Include the emergency number (911) and the telephone numbers of your baby's doctor, dentist, a neighbor, and a close relative in case you can't be reached. Also include your other children's names and any allergies. Laminate it and put it by the telephone. Now when you go out, you will only need to write the address, telephone number, and place where you will be.

Day 38

Give your baby a soothing tummy massage. Start with both hands close together at the lower part of his torso. Slide your hands over his tummy and across his chest.

Slide them down either side to complete the circle. Do
this four or five times. When you massage your baby,
smile and talk lovingly as you use smooth, gentle strokes.

Day 39

Help your baby practice tracking (following an object)
with her eyes. Hold a rattle above her eyes about ten
inches away. Wait for her to focus. Gently shake the rattle
and slowly move it a little to the left and then to the right.
Let her follow the rattle with her eyes. Expand the arc
more as she is able to follow it. Eventually she will be able
to track her eyes 180 degrees.

Day 40

Babies are irresistible, but they can take up a lot of
time and use up every ounce of energy you have. That's
why it's important to keep your husband/wife relationship
a priority. Try spending ten minutes a day talking together
after dinner. Sit your baby in his infant seat so he is close
by, but let your focus be on each other. Your marriage
relationship needs to be nurtured and cared for; it can't
run on autopilot indefinitely.

Day 41

Babies are so wonderful to touch. You probably do
not need to be told this, but caress and kiss your baby
often. Play with her toes, stroke her hair, rub her legs,

razz her tummy, blow on her fingers, and kiss her cheeks. Your gentle touch will communicate your love for her.

Day 42

This is a good time to start a bedtime routine that can be used at nap time too. One example would be to change her diaper, read her a book, sing a lullaby, and then lay her in her crib with a pacifier. Having a routine helps her body wind down and signals to her that it is sleep time. It will also help her learn to fall asleep on her own.

Reflections on the Week

She is clothed with strength and dignity...Her children arise and call her blessed; her husband also, and he praises her: "Many women do noble things, but you surpass them all."

PROVERBS 31:25,28-29

God has given each of you some special abilities; be sure to use them to help each other, passing on to others God's many kinds of blessings.

1 PETER 4:10 TLB

The Most Important Job

You have the most important job in the world—you are a mother. From the moment you knew your little baby was on the way, your life was forever changed for the better. God has given you the unequaled privilege to love, nurture, and care for your precious child. It is a humbling responsibility and an incomparable blessing.

You may not feel as though you are accomplishing anything great, but as a mother you are making a permanent difference in your child's life. A price tag cannot be put on the value of rocking your baby, singing her lullabies, praying for her, stimulating her intellect, selflessly caring for her every need, and loving her the way no one else could ever do. Your presence brings warmth, comfort, protection, and safety to her life.

God wants you to look beyond the mundane, repetitive tasks you perform daily and instead see His vision of motherhood—a divine calling, a position of influence, and an incredible responsibility. Mothers impact the world in a positive way by raising the next generation of leaders. The fruits of your labor will last for generations to come because a loving mother's influence never fades away.

Dear God, thank You that You have allowed me to be a mother. Thank You that I am never alone in my responsibilities as a mom. I know that You are with me wherever I go and in whatever I do. Sometimes I feel as though I am not getting a thing done. Help me to see my job as a mother the way You see it—the most important vocation a woman can ever have! Please help me remember that my job is significant and eternally important. Amen.

Week 7

Day 43

Take your baby out for a daily walk if the weather permits. It is good for both of you to get some fresh air, see a change of scenery, and hear new sounds. It might even give you the opportunity to meet other new moms who are out walking their babies. On top of it all, walking is a great aerobic exercise for you!

Day 44

Stop back problems before they start. When you pick up your baby, hold in your tummy, keep your back straight, and bend your knees. Use your leg muscles to lift instead of relying on your back muscles.

Day 45

Let your baby know how you feel about him. Tell him, "_____, I'm so happy you're my little baby," or turn your feelings into a rhyme. Try this:

I feel great	*(point to self)*
When you're with me	*(point to baby)*
You are as special	*(clap his hands)*
As can be!	*(move his hands outward)*

Day 46

If you are nursing, start giving your baby a bottle once or twice a week so she won't reject it later. This will allow you a little freedom if you want to go out and won't be home in time for her next feeding.

Day 47

Give your baby a chest massage. Place your right hand on his right hip. Move your hand across his body over to his left shoulder. Immediately place your left hand on baby's left hip and move your hand up and over his right shoulder. It will be like making an X across his torso. Repeat five times at a slow, steady pace.

Day 48

Stay in tune with your baby as you play with her. When she loses interest (turns her head, fusses, or cries), stop your play session. Babies have very short attention spans and can easily become overstimulated. Be a good student of your baby. Get to know what calms her, what excites her, and what engages her.

Day 49

Let your baby lie on a blanket or sit in her infant seat by the fireplace (at a safe distance) to watch the light flicker from the flames. This beautiful light show will mesmerize her.

Reflections on the Week

Do you not know that your body is a temple of the Holy Spirit, who is in you, whom you have received from God?... Therefore honor God with your body.

1 CORINTHIANS 6:19-20

I praise you because I am fearfully and wonderfully made; your works are wonderful, I know that full well. My frame was not hidden from you when I was made in the secret place.

PSALM 139:14-15

Take Care of Your Body

During this season of your life, you will find it so easy to place your baby's needs before your own. This selfless giving is a part of motherhood, but it shouldn't be done to the detriment of your health. You need to refuel your body with healthy foods and nutritious snacks so you will have the energy necessary to care for your baby. You need to drink plenty of water to stay hydrated. Drink a glassful every time you sit down to nurse or feed your baby. You will feel better about yourself and your outlook on life will improve when you make sure your body is well cared for.

Even though you know it's important, you may often feel too tired to exercise. You might ask, "How can I possibly exercise when I am already exhausted?" Exercise, however, will give you the stamina and strength to adjust to your new life as a mother. Exercise will speed up your recovery from childbirth, improve your mental attitude, and help you get back to your prepregnancy shape. Try to find fifteen minutes in your day to exercise. Some days take your baby on a brisk walk. Other days do calisthenics at home as you interact with your baby next to you. I have found that doing push-ups, abdominal crunches (sit ups), and leg lunges pretty much cover all the main muscle groups and will help tone your muscles. Occasionally try to exercise alone after your husband gets home. Half the battle of exercising is just getting started. As the Nike advertisement says, "Just do it!"

*D*ear God, sometimes I feel as though I am running on empty. Help me to take better care of myself. Help me to know what foods to stock in my refrigerator and pantry that will give my body the nutrients You designed it to run on. Please also help me to find fifteen minutes in my day to exercise. As hard as it is to start, I know I always feel better after I have exercised.

Thank You that I can bring all my concerns to You and know that You will help me creatively resolve each one. Amen.

Week 8

Day 50

Your baby loves to hear you sing. Sing "The Itsy Bitsy Spider" to him while you do the hand motions on his tummy.

The itsy bitsy spider climbed up the water-spout	*(walk your fingers up his tummy)*
Down came the rain	*(drag your fingers down his tummy)*
And washed the spider out	*(smooth your hands across his tummy)*
Out came the sun	*(bounce your fingers up his tummy)*
And dried up all the rain	*(slide your hands down his tummy)*
So the itsy bitsy spider climbed up the spout again	*(walk your fingers up his tummy)*

Day 51

Play peekaboo and give your legs a workout at the same time. Hold onto your baby's crib and smile at her.

Squat down or do a plié (knees out to the side) until you can't see your baby's face. Stand back up and say, "peek-aboo!" Repeat several times throughout the day.

Day 52

Put your baby in a baby swing so he can watch what is going on around him. Swings are especially helpful to calm him during a fussy time or to allow you and your husband to have an uninterrupted meal together. However, don't always use the swing as a tool to get him to fall asleep. It is better for him to learn to fall asleep on his own naturally without any mechanical devices.

Day 53

Give your baby daily opportunities to strengthen her neck and back muscles. Lay her on your chest facedown while you lay down. She will lift her head to see your face. You can also lay her on her tummy and shake a rattle in front of her face. Slowly lift the rattle just a little to encourage her to lift her head and shoulders to watch it move. Lifting that heavy head is hard work!

Day 54

You may be more of a free spirit who likes change and variety, but babies like structure and order. Try to do things the same way each time you do them and have a predictable routine to your day. All babies need this, but it is especially important for "difficult" or "high-need" babies. Developing a routine where the same events occur in sequence helps babies know what to expect next and develops a sense of trust.

Day 55

Put a moving musical mobile on your baby's crib or changing table. He will love to watch and listen to it. The mobile will also help him learn to track moving objects with his eyes.

Day 56

Watching your baby receive her immunization shots can often be more traumatic for you than for her. Here are a few tips to make it easier for both of you. When you bring your baby in for her checkup, have her wear an outfit that is easy to get on and off. After the doctor is finished examining her, get her almost completely dressed except for her leg (or wherever they will be giving the immunization). Give her a pacifier to help her relax so the shot is less painful. Lean over her to give a hug, placing your face close to hers (now you don't have to watch!). As soon as the nurse puts the Band-Aid on, you can hold and comfort her.

Reflections on the Week

Let the wife see that she respects and reverences her husband [that she notices

*him, regards him, honors him, prefers
him, venerates, and esteems him; and
that she defers to him, praises him, and
loves and admires him exceedingly].*

EPHESIANS 5:32 AMP

*May you rejoice in the wife of your youth...
may you ever be captivated by her love.*

PROVERBS 5:18-19

Loving Your Husband

You have entered a new love affair. Who would have
ever guessed how passionately, how intensely you would
love your baby? Every sweet part of him arouses your
senses. It is a love affair with a person who adores you,
who thinks you are the best thing going, who smiles at
you whenever he can catch your eye. Baby love can be
intoxicating, yet you must not forget your first love—your
husband.

A new baby can draw parents closer together as you
marvel at this new child you have brought into the world.
Oftentimes, though, your marriage gets unwittingly put
on the back burner as you bask in the joy and time
required for this new love. Yet, your marriage is the
cornerstone of your family. You need to be careful not to
let it die from slow neglect; you must protect it. Your
effectiveness as a parent can only be as strong as the relationship you have with your husband. A strong marriage
is what will provide a secure, stable home for your
children.

Plan time to be together. Think about him during the day. As antiquated as it may sound, freshen up before your husband gets home. Send him a note at work. Plan a date. Ask him how his day was instead of immediately bombarding him with the events of your day the minute he walks in the door. Creatively bring romance back into your marriage. It may not be easy to find the time to do any of these. You may not even feel like doing them, but investing in your marriage has to be one of your top priorities.

Dear God, I do love my husband so much and am very thankful for everything he does. I admit, though, that I often give all my energy, all my sweet caresses, and all my tender words to my little baby. Sometimes there is not much left over for my husband. Lord, help me to show my husband my love for him on a daily basis. Help me to not take him for granted. Let me remember that I can only be as good a mother as I am a wife. Thank You for bringing this wonderful man into my life. Amen.

Week 9

Day 57

When you approach your baby to pick him up, smile and speak softly to get his attention. He will soon begin to smile and coo when he sees you. When he does this, it is his way of communicating, so respond by smiling and speaking to him again. Your smile is worth a thousand words. Rejoice in your first conversation with your baby!

Day 58

Give your baby a foot massage. How could you resist those sweet little feet? Slide your thumb along her sole from heel to toe several times, and then gently massage those little toes one by one. Point and flex her feet, then gently rotate her ankles in a circle. Marvel at the beauty of God's creation as you massage your baby's feet.

Day 59

Even if your baby is cranky, the house is a mess, and none of your clothes fit, slow down for a second and appreciate just how truly blessed you are. Count your blessings one by one, beginning with your wonderful little bundle of joy.

Day 60

Strengthen your chest and triceps while kissing your baby. Lay him on the floor on his back. Get on your hands and knees over your baby and do push-ups. Give your baby a kiss as you go down, but only do this if you know you are strong enough to push yourself back up!

Your Baby Is Two Months Old!

Day 61

Lay your baby on her back and play "Pat-a-Cake" with her. Move her hands to do the hand motions.

Pat-a-cake, pat-a-cake   *(clap hands)*
baker's man

Bake me a cake as fast   *(clap hands)*
as you can

Roll it   *(roll hands)*

And toss it   *(open hands to the sides)*

| *And mark it with a* | *(draw a "B" on baby's* |
| *"B"* | *chest with her hand)* |

| *Put it in the oven for* | *(point hands to baby)* |
| _____ | |

| *And me* | *(point to self)* |

It's time for your baby's two-month checkup.

Day 62

Start a lifetime love of reading. Read to your baby from the very beginning. Read short, colorful board books while you hold him in your lap. Read with animation and expression. He will love listening to the sound of your voice, feeling your warm embrace, and seeing the brightly colored pictures.

Day 63

Here's an easy way to start toning your thighs. Hold your baby close to your chest. Stand in front of the couch with your back to it. Pull your tummy in and push your bottom back while bending your knees as if you were going to sit down. When your toes start to lift off the ground, squeeze your bottom and return to the starting position. Do this exercise several times throughout the day.

Reflections on the Week

Be joyful always; pray continually; give thanks in all circumstances, for this is God's will for you in Christ Jesus.

1 THESSALONIANS 5:16-18

Do not be anxious about anything, but in everything, by prayer and petition, with thanksgiving, present your requests to God. And the peace of God, which transcends all understanding, will guard your hearts and your minds in Christ Jesus.

PHILIPPIANS 4:6-7

Talking with God

When we pray, we come into God's presence and have a conversation with Him. We don't need to be in a certain place or use fancy words or even be on our knees. We simply need to share our hearts. The power of prayer does not come from the words we use, but from God Himself. He is our loving heavenly Father, and everything we say to Him, everything that is going on in our lives, is important to Him. When we pray, we receive peace from knowing that He is in control.

Prayer is how we build a relationship with God. He can hear our thoughts, but He wants us to talk directly with Him. He wants us to be honest, open, and sincere with Him. This is how we build relationships with friends, and this is what God desires from us. As we begin spending more time with Him, we become more like Him. As we begin thanking God for all of our blessings, it changes our attitude. It changes our perspective on life.

Talk to the Lord as you go about your day. He longs to hear from you. You don't need to spend an hour in prayer every morning to have a relationship with Him. God created motherhood; He understands how much time it takes to care for babies. God just wants you to cast your cares upon Him and sing praises to Him as you go about the sacred work of mothering.

Each of the devotions in this book ends with a short prayer. They are prayers that speak from the desire of my heart and hopefully yours. If you aren't used to praying, you can pray these prayers simply as they are or use them as a springboard to a longer conversation with God.

Dear Heavenly Father, thank You that You are always available. Thank You that You will answer each one of my prayers according to what is best for me. Remind me to turn to You and lay all my troubles and concerns at Your feet. It is so comforting and reassuring to know that You are in control. Nothing is too difficult for You to handle! Thank You for hearing my prayers. Amen.

Week 10

Day 64

Hold your baby on your lap. Lean forward slowly as you say, "ahhh." Gently touch your forehead to his forehead and say, "boo." You will be making a continuous "ahhboo" sound as you play this game.

Day 65

Show your baby how delighted you are to see her by saying hello whenever you greet her. Try to smile when you look and talk to your baby, even if she doesn't smile often. She will begin smiling more just by imitating you. Reinforce her smiles with more smiles and talking.

Day 66

Your baby not only needs playtime with you, he also needs quiet time by himself to relax. You do not always need to be stimulating and interacting with him during every waking moment. Sit him in his bouncy chair to look out a window or lay him on a blanket to look at some toys.

Day 67

Sit your baby in her infant seat. Stand behind her and whisper her name near her right ear until she turns to your voice. Next whisper in her left ear and let her turn to your voice. She is beginning to coordinate her vision and hearing as she turns to see the source of her favorite sound, your voice!

Day 68

Give your baby a leg and arm massage. Start at the ankle and use a gentle wringing motion, circling your hands in opposite directions all the way up to the groin. Do this three times on each leg. Use the same motion on his arm by starting at his wrist and working your way up to his armpit.

Day 69

Sing "Head, Shoulders, Knees and Toes." Touch your baby's body parts as you name them.

Head, shoulders, knees and toes, knees and toes

Head, shoulders, knees and toes, knees and toes

My eyes and ears and mouth and nose

Head, shoulders, knees and toes, knees and toes

Day 70

Do not forget about your marriage relationship. Find a sitter you are comfortable with and try to go on a date with your husband once a week. It can be as short and simple as a walk through the park, getting an ice cream cone, or going out for a cup of coffee. It is easy to get so caught up in meeting the needs of your baby that you can unintentionally end up neglecting each other. Your baby's security will be fostered by the love she feels between you and your husband.

Reflections on the Week

I tell you the truth, whatever you did for one of the least of these [children] of mine, you did for me.

MATTHEW 25:40

Serve wholeheartedly, as if you were serving the Lord, not men, because you know that the Lord will reward everyone for whatever good he does.

EPHESIANS 6:7-8

Motherhood Is a Ministry

Motherhood is a ministry, an opportunity, a calling, and a position of great influence. Mothers shape the next generation and impact society more than any other profession. There is no other career so important, so precious, so urgent, so rewarding. Often our culture devalues the importance of motherhood. If you have left a career to become a full-time mom, you may feel uncomfortable answering the question, "And what do you do?" No longer is it easy to put into words exactly what you do all day. If you can catch a glimpse of God's vision of motherhood, however, it will lift you above the world's view that motherhood is a thankless, boring, and intellectually unstimulating occupation.

You are using your time, talent, skills, energy, and intelligence to raise mature, respectful, morally conscious, loving, responsible, emotionally stable children. Mothers build secure homes, develop character, strengthen family relationships, set an example of godly living, impart knowledge and wisdom, give spiritual training, and instill values. What a job description! You will influence few people as intimately and profoundly as you do your children. What you are doing has lasting value. Your work matters to God. Parenting is one of the greatest ministry opportunities.

*D*ear God, thank You for the privilege of being called a mother. I love my new "job." Help me to catch a glimpse of Your vision of motherhood. Help me to see that what I do today and in the years to come will have an impact on future generations and, in turn, the world. Help me put just as much, if not more, energy and devotion into this career as I would any other. Amen.

Week 11

Day 71

When it is bedtime, use a soothing voice, loving words, and a gentle touch. Stroke her face and say something like, "Goodnight sweet _____. Mommy loves you." Let her fall asleep feeling loved.

Day 72

An activity gym is a great investment to buy or borrow if you do not already have one. Let your baby lie underneath it and watch the dangling toys. He will soon begin to start swatting at the toys with his hands. This is great practice for eye-hand coordination.

Day 73

Help get your abdominal muscles back in shape and let your baby enjoy a ride. Lie on your back with your knees bent. Lay your baby on her tummy against your shins while holding her arms and back securely. Raise your ankles up and down fifteen times. Next raise your lower legs so your shins are parallel to the ground. Lift your head and shoulders while keeping your lower back on the floor. Do as many crunches as you can. She will enjoy this form of peekaboo as your face appears and disappears with each crunch.

Day 74

Exercise your baby's legs. Lay him on his back and cup his feet in your hands. Sing:

Up, down, up down   *(move his legs up and down together)*

Swing them all around!   *(swing his legs in a circle)*

Day 75

Make sure your baby knows now and always that she is truly one of God's greatest gifts, a valuable treasure! Tell her how thankful you are that God gave her to you. Tell her what a blessing she is to you and your family.

Day 76

Encourage your baby to use both sides of his body. Often a baby will favor one side and will always look in that direction. Play with him in ways that will encourage him to look the other way. Try laying him on his changing table in the direction that causes him to look at you from the side he favors least. This will allow him to strengthen his neck muscles on both sides and keep his head development symmetrical.

Day 77

When your baby starts waking up happy (instead of immediately crying), say, "There's my happy girl! What a nice smile. You woke up with such a happy spirit." You can begin encouraging a happy disposition from the very beginning by offering her positive reinforcement. Set your baby up for success by going in to get her while she is still content instead of waiting for her to start crying. This doesn't mean you need to run in and get her the minute she opens her eyes, though. She might be happy to lie in her crib and look around for ten minutes. Just try to go in before she becomes distressed.

Reflections on the Week

The LORD does not look at the things man looks at. Man looks at the outward appearance, but the LORD looks at the heart.

1 SAMUEL 16:7

Your beauty should not come from out-ward adornment, such as braided hair and the wearing of gold jewelry and fine clothes. Instead, it should be that of your inner self, the unfading beauty of a

*gentle and quiet spirit, which is of great
worth in God's sight.*

1 Peter 3:3-4

Looking Good!

How are you looking today? Sometimes mornings, afternoons, and evenings all seem to run together, and you may never get around to fixing your hair, putting on a little makeup, or getting out of your sweats. When you do take the time to look presentable, doesn't it usually make you feel better about yourself? This in turn often can improve your attitude towards life.

Your baby is now better able to entertain himself on a blanket long enough for you to make yourself look presentable. You don't need to make a fashion statement, but you can have a clean, attractive appearance. Wear clothes that are flattering yet comfortable enough to get down on the floor and play. Look for something a step above your husband's dowdy sweatpants and several steps below "dry clean only." If you are not back into your prepregnancy clothes yet, splurge on one or two new outfits that look good on you. Shop at a discount or second-hand store to get a good deal because hopefully they won't fit for long.

On those days when you just can't get it together, remember your outer beauty does not determine your value. What is more important is the inner beauty of a kind and loving heart. This is what you must spend time cultivating. A truly beautiful woman is recognized more by her attitude and disposition than by her hairstyle or wardrobe collection.

Dear God, as a woman, I tend to feel better about myself when I feel attractive. Help me to find the time to be able to do at least some basic grooming. I want to look presentable for my own self-confidence and for my husband's benefit. I thank You that You don't look at my outward appearance, but You value me just because I am Your dearly beloved child. Help me cultivate a radiant inner beauty. Amen.

Week 12

Day 78

A ball will become one of your baby's favorite toys. You can start playing ball with him now by laying him on his tummy. Roll a colorful ball in front of him. Encourage him to follow the moving ball with his eyes. It won't be long before he is rolling the ball back to you!

Day 79

Your baby will enjoy hearing you say this little poem and will begin to joyfully anticipate the tickle at the end.

Round and round the garden	*(trace circles on his tummy with your finger)*
Goes the teddy bear	*(trace circles on his tummy with your finger)*
One step, two steps	*(walk your fingers up his chest)*
Tickle him under there!	*(gently tickle him under his chin)*

Day 80

Show your baby lots of affection and attention before she cries for it. You are establishing a solid foundation for a trusting relationship as you respond lovingly to her needs. She is learning that you will always love her and be there for her, not just when she demands it.

Day 81

Make sure your baby gets some time on his tummy several times a day. This will give him the opportunity to hold his head up, push up on his arms, and rock on his belly. You can join him and strengthen your back at the same time. Lie on your stomach facing your baby's head. (You should be lying on the floor head-to-head with your baby.) Extend your arms out in front of you so they are resting on either side of your baby. Lift your head, arms, and shoulders off the ground and smile at him. Now you can appreciate what hard work it is for him to do this!

Day 82

Play a game by imitating your baby's sounds (siblings will love to do this!). When your baby coos, coo back; when she gurgles, gurgle back. The more you respond, the more your baby will vocalize and smile. Every sound she makes is a building block in her speech development. The sounds will become a combination of sounds, then words, and eventually sentences.

Day 83

Your baby loves to hear you sing, and this activity can turn your house into a joyful home. Make up little songs as you go about your day. Many things can be sung to the tune of "Here We Go Round the Mulberry Bush." For example, "This is the way we put on our socks...clean up our room...wash our tummy...fold the clothes," and so on.

Day 84

On a ninety-minute cassette tape, make an audio recording of your baby's sounds for a maximum of five minutes. Record him cooing and even crying. Say how old your baby is on it. Every three months add a few more minutes to the tape, verbally recording the age each time. By the time your baby is five years old, you will have a history on tape of your child's speech development. It will be fun for you and your child to listen to it when he is older.

Reflections on the Week

Work hard and cheerfully at all you do, just as though you were working for the Lord...He is the one you are really working for.

COLOSSIANS 3:23-24 TLB

I can do all things through Him who strengthens me.

PHILIPPIANS 4:13 NASB

Managing Your Home

Your house will probably never look perfect and be completely picked up with young children around, but it can be clean and relatively orderly. As you manage what God has given you, you can make your home a happy, welcoming place. You don't need a house to have a home. Wherever you live can be made into a home when love, laughter, and joy reside there. Your home, however, can't be a peaceful oasis if it is always a mess, piles of laundry are everywhere, and the refrigerator is empty. You shouldn't try to achieve decorator showroom status, but your home should be comfortably clean and picked up.

Ideally it would be nice to have a housekeeper come to help clean during the first few months after your baby has arrived. Financially that may not be possible, especially if you are down to only one income. Your husband can and should help, but usually the bulk of housework will remain with you. Here are some tips that have helped me run my home more efficiently:

Laundry—Place two laundry containers side by side (one for colors, one for whites) so laundry is sorted as it is tossed in. Place a load in the washer every night (or every other night) before you go to bed. Turn it on first thing in the morning. Put away the clothes as soon as you take them out of the dryer instead of leaving them in a pile to fold later. One load of laundry is pretty easy to put away, and then you are done for the day (with the laundry anyway!).

Keeping the house picked up—First of all, de-clutter. Get rid of everything you don't use or need. Find a place for everything else. When you are finished using something, put it away. "A place for everything and everything in its place" really works and saves time in the long run. This next bit of advice will sound like your mother speaking, but make your bed. It's the biggest thing in your room, and if it looks tidy, seventy percent of your bedroom will look clean. Give the house one final pick up before you go to bed at night so you can have the pleasure of waking up to a clean house.

Cleaning—Set up a schedule so you only have one cleaning job a day to do. Try to complete it in thirty minutes. A half hour a day of cleaning isn't too bad, is it? You might divide your chores like this: Monday—kitchen; Tuesday—bathrooms; Wednesday—dust; Thursday—vacuum; and Friday—paperwork and bills.

Dear Lord, trying to take care of both a home and a baby can be overwhelming. It takes so much planning and organization. Help me to implement some of these tips so I can better manage my time. Help me also to remember that my family is more important than housework. Chores are just necessary interruptions to the real work of raising my child and loving my husband. Amen.

Week 13

Day 85

Turn on some slow music and give your baby some exercise time with you. Do each of these exercises three or four times slowly and gently while she lies on her back:

1. Hold your baby's hands. Open her arms to the sides then close them across her chest.

2. Hold your baby's lower legs. Bend her knees up, and then lower them down straight.

3. Raise one arm above your baby's head while bringing the other arm down to her side; alternate arms.

Day 86

Help your baby hold a rattle by opening up her fist and sliding the rattle in before she closes her hand. She will begin to realize that when she moves her hand, the rattle makes a sound. She will find this new discovery of cause and effect fascinating.

Day 87

Lay your baby on her back. Let her grasp your finger. Pull her gently onto her side. Then let her roll back. This helps prepare her for what it will feel like when she rolls over on her own. She will probably roll over by herself for the first time when you least expect it. Be prepared and don't leave her alone on the bed, couch, or changing table.

Day 88

Your baby is beginning to like to explore things with his mouth, yet he does not have the manual dexterity to hold things in his mouth by himself. To help him, cover your finger with a clean cloth diaper and let him chew on it. The diaper is soft, it is a different texture, and it will protect his mouth from your fingernails.

Day 89

You have fallen deeply in love with your baby, and she has fallen in love with you. Her face lights up when she sees you. She stares at you, waiting to get your attention. When you respond, she bursts into a big smile. What a wonderful time in your baby's life this is!

Your Baby Is Three Months Old!

Day 90

Sing "The Ants Go Marching" as you exercise your baby's legs. Do the leg motions gently.

The ants go marching one by one. Hurrah! Hurrah!	*(hold his ankles and bend his legs up and down in a marching motion)*
The ants go marching one by one. Hurrah! Hurrah!	*(repeat)*
The ants go marching one by one	*(repeat)*
The little one stopped to suck his thumb	*(repeat)*
And they all go marching	*(repeat)*
Down to the ground to get out of the rain	*(swing legs together side to side)*
Boom, boom	*(lift ankles up and down)*
Boom	*(kiss his tummy)*

Day 91

Don't feel you need to always be the one initiating and directing play. Spend time just enjoying your baby and watching him "perform." Follow his lead. Show your pleasure by kissing him, clapping your hands, and speaking words of encouragement.

Reflections on the Week

If one falls down, his friend can help him up. But pity the man who falls and has no one to help him up!

ECCLESIASTES 4:10

A friend loves at all times.

PROVERBS 17:17

Good Friends

Being a new mom can be an isolating experience. Many of your friends may be at work or don't have children, so you have less in common with them now. Yet as a new mother, you need close friendships, especially with other women who have young babies. Friends who can say, "I know just how you feel," who can offer encouragement, and who can share ideas. Having other mom friends will help you keep things in perspective.

Being outgoing enough to meet new moms may require you to go outside your comfort zone. Remember, however, these women probably would like to meet a new friend just as much as you would! Strike up a conversation with women at the park, in your neighborhood, or in the church nursery. Not everyone you meet will be your best friend, but everyone is a potential friend with something to offer. When you find someone you click with, invite her over for coffee to get to know her better. Find a common interest and build on it. Over time, your friendships will deepen as you begin to share more of yourself.

Some days it's just too hectic to get out of the house to get together with a friend, but you can still use the telephone. You need to connect with other women on a regular basis. You can't expect your husband to meet all your emotional needs and fully understand the challenges you face. Even if you have a great relationship with your husband, you still need friendships with other women.

Dear Lord, some days I am so lonely. I don't have any close friends with babies. Please help me find some like-minded friends, maybe even a kindred spirit. Give me the courage to introduce myself to other moms instead of waiting to be approached by them. Help me find a group of women who can walk with me through this wonderful yet sometimes wearisome journey of motherhood. Amen.

The Second
Three Months

A Bundle of Smiles

Oh, the smiles that are
halos of heaven,

Shedding sunshine of love
on my face.

CHARLES M. DICKINSON

Week 14

Day 92

Motivate your baby to roll over by putting an interesting object on one side of him as he lies on his back. As he turns a little, help him roll over all the way.

Day 93

Help your baby learn to do the "Hokey Pokey." Let her lie on her back while you gently move her arms and legs.

You put your right arm in	*(put her arm to her side)*
You put your right arm out	*(hold her arm out)*
You put your right arm in	*(put her arm to her side)*
And you shake it all about	*(gently shake her arm)*
You do the Hokey Pokey	*(hold her hands out front and move them up and down)*

And you turn yourself around   *(move arms together in a circle)*

That's what it's all about!   *(clap her hands together)*

Day 94

Don't forget to take several pictures of your baby each month. He is changing so quickly. This is especially important if this is not your first child. Make sure you take some pictures of just your baby—without any siblings. You might want to take a picture each month in the same chair so you can see how much he has grown. When you get a really good picture, date the back of it and put it with his baby book. When you get a chance to work on his baby book, everything will be easy to find. You might also want to keep your negatives at a relative's house in case your pictures get damaged. Keep your doubles in a special place because he will need pictures for school projects when he is older.

Day 95

When talking to your baby, refer to yourself as "Mommy" (or "Daddy"). Use your baby's name instead of using pronouns. For example, "Now Mommy is going to wash _____'s face."

Day 96

When you check on your sleeping baby, pray over her. Praise God for the gift of this child. Pray for her safety, her health, and her spiritual development.

Day 97

Allow fifteen more minutes than you think you will need to get ready when you are going somewhere. This helps budget time for changing a last minute diaper, looking for a lost item, or answering the phone—all the inevitable things that can turn a simple outing into a major ordeal.

Day 98

Talk with your child rather than at him. Pause as you talk or ask questions to give your baby a chance to respond. He may coo or gurgle to participate in the conversation.

Reflections on the Week

A cheerful heart is good medicine.

PROVERBS 17:22

The LORD has done great things for us, and we are filled with joy.

PSALM 126:3

A Cheerful Disposition

One of the greatest gifts you can give to your children is a cheerful, optimistic attitude that always looks for the good in others. As a mother, you set the tone for your home. Bless your family by making sure there is plenty of laughter, joy, and fun. Smile often when you speak to your children and husband. Greet them with a hug when they come home. Children thrive in an atmosphere of cheerfulness. It is contagious. Your pleasant disposition will rub off on your children, and then they in turn will spread their joy to others.

My daughter's preschool teacher was a great example to me in this area. She was always smiling and genuinely happy to see each child. She made up little songs as she interacted with the children. You couldn't help but feel happy in her presence.

You might not have a naturally perky personality like hers, but you can sing and laugh and not take things too seriously. Look at the positive side of things; encourage rather than criticize. When your children spill drinks or accidentally break things, you can respond with patience and forgiveness rather than anger.

You can have this inner joy and peace from knowing God and trusting in Him, instead of letting your circumstances determine your attitude. Walking closely with God helps put daily challenges in perspective.

*D*ear God, thank You for the joy that comes only from knowing You. Help me share that joy with others. I know my disposition sets the tone for my whole family. Help me build a home that is filled with laughter, joy, enthusiasm, and fun. Amen.

Week 15

Day 99

Take time to just "soak up" your baby. Hold her close, kiss her downy hair, nuzzle her soft cheeks, and gaze into her beautiful eyes. Tell her how much you love her. Savor the moment. Store it in your memory.

Day 100

Greet your baby with a happy song when you get him out of the crib in the morning. Try:

> *Good morning, good morning*
> *And how do you do?*
> *Good morning, good morning*
> *I'm fine, how are you?*

Day 101

Watch for times when your baby smiles at you. Be especially affectionate then, telling her how much you like to see her smile. Continually praise her as she gradually smiles more and more. This will help her cultivate a happy disposition.

Day 102

Think about holding your tummy in when you are holding your baby. It is a good isometric exercise, it will help improve your posture, and it will help support your back. This is especially important as your baby gets heavier!

Day 103

Play all different types of music for your baby, especially classical. Some studies have shown that listening to classical music can help your baby's brain develop. If nothing else, it has the power to calm your baby and provide a peaceful home environment.

Day 104

Lay your baby on her back. Walk slowly around her as you sing a favorite song. Encourage her to follow you and your voice with her eyes. She will love to watch the show, and you will never have a more attentive audience!

Day 105

Play peekaboo with your baby. Start by just covering your face with your hands for a moment saying, "Where's Mommy?" then remove your hands and say, "Here I am!" or "Peekaboo!" As your baby gets older, you can use a blanket to hide your face and then eventually progress to hiding his face with a blanket. This game teaches your baby that even though your face disappears for a moment, you are still there.

Reflections on the Week

The LORD your God is with you, he is mighty to save. He will take great delight in you, he will quiet you with his love, he will rejoice over you with singing.

ZEPHANIAH 3:17

He tends his flock like a shepherd: He gathers the lambs in his arms and carries them close to his heart; he gently leads those that have young.

ISAIAH 40:11

Making Time for God

God gently leads those with young children even when there seems to be no time to spend with Him. He understands and extends His grace, yet we are the ones who suffer when we don't spend time with Him. There is power in God's Word and in prayer. I don't know how to explain it, but I can always tell the difference when I spend time with God and when I don't. Have you noticed it too? We regain our perspective. We have the power to persevere. Things seem to fall into place more easily, and if they don't, we are not as upset about it. Spending time reading God's Word and praying to Him is like getting our batteries recharged.

You know it's important, but how do you find the time to do it? At this point in your life, you probably won't have long stretches of uninterrupted time, but you don't have to stop everything to be with God; you just need to be consciously walking with Him. You can read the Bible while you nurse. You can tape Bible verses to your bathroom mirror, meditating on them and then putting them into action in your life. Listen to Christian radio programs as you run errands, pray as you fold laundry, and play praise music as you prepare dinner. Just relax and enjoy being in God's presence throughout the day.

*D*ear God, I feel guilty because I don't spend as much time as I would like with You. I can't even remember the last time I opened my Bible, yet I do know I need You. I can't become more like You if I am not spending time with You. I can't benefit from Your wisdom if I'm not reading the Bible. Help me to find creative ways to talk with You and read Your Word as I go about my day. Amen.

Week 16

Day 106

When you begin to feel as though you will never have your whole house picked up and looking nice all at once again, remember this saying:

> *Blessed is the house*
> *That is clean enough to be healthy,*
> *Messy enough to be happy,*
> *And where love abounds.*

Day 107

Tell your baby often how much you love her and how happy you are that God gave her to you. He picked the very best baby just for you!

Day 108

Pull your baby up to a sitting position with his hands a couple of times a day. As he gains better neck control, he will eventually be able to keep his head in line with his body instead of dropping it back.

Day 109

Your baby prefers to look at bright colors now, so wear a colorful scarf (or one of your husband's old ties) and lean over her so she can reach it. She will enjoy batting her arms at the scarf, watching it move, and seeing your excited facial expressions up close.

Day 110

Sit your baby on your lap. Give him a big piece of wrapping paper to play with. He will enjoy watching it move, seeing how he can change its shape, and hearing it crunch. Be careful, however, not to let him chew on the paper because of inks that may be in it.

Day 111

Stand with your baby in front of a mirror. Point to her reflection. Touch and name different body parts as you both look into the mirror. Encourage your baby to touch her reflection. She will begin to smile and vocalize at her image.

Day 112

Gently bounce your baby on your knees, singing to the tune of "Here We Go Round the Mulberry Bush."

This is the way _____ rides,
_____ rides, _____ rides

This is the way my baby rides

Bouncity, bouncity, bounce

Reflections on the Week

Children's children are a crown to the aged, and parents are the pride of their children.

PROVERBS 17:6

Listen, my son, to your father's instruction and do not forsake your mother's teaching.

PROVERBS 1:8

The Love of a Grandparent

What a blessing grandparents are to children. They can spoil them a little and love them a lot. They are genuinely interested in your child. Grandparents have time to get down on the floor and play. They are not in a rush because they aren't worried about getting something else done. They are unashamedly your baby's biggest fans. Grandparents love their grandchildren without any demands or expectations.

What a blessing your baby's grandparents are to you. They can appreciate all the cute little things your baby does and says. A grandparent will wholeheartedly enjoy hearing about things that may bore or seem like bragging to a friend. If you are open to it, your children's grandparents can offer you much wisdom in your parenting. They speak from years of experience.

Grandparents build a child's sense of extended family. When children spend time with their grandparents, they learn that family is important. It is your job to nurture this relationship. Plan visits and let your baby "talk" to them on the telephone so she can hear her grandparents' voices. Let her spend time alone with them. Keep photographs of your parents displayed where your child can see them. Talk to your baby about her grandparents with excitement and fondness. Nurturing this relationship now will bring many blessings to your child in the future as this friendship blossoms.

Dear Father, thank You for my baby's grandparents. I love to watch their enthusiastic faces as they play with her. Help me to creatively nurture this relationship. Thank You for the wisdom gained by experience that my parents and in-laws can offer me. Help me to be humble and appreciate receiving it. Amen.

Week 17

Day 113

Your baby can see different colors and objects at a distance now. This opens up a whole new world for him to enjoy. He will begin to laugh at unexpected sights and sounds that he encounters. Have fun playing with him as he discovers more and more about the world around him.

Day 114

When you play with your baby, remember that her reactions to things are much slower than yours. Slow your pace to hers. When you talk to her, give her time (maybe ten to fifteen seconds) to answer with a sound. When you hand her a toy, wait patiently until she begins the painstaking process of reaching for it. When you smile at her, give her a chance to smile back.

Day 115

Your baby learns by using all of his senses. Make use of this as you play with him. Try using a straw to blow air on different parts of his body. He will love the tickly sensation.

Day 116

Your baby is beginning to reach out and grab things. When you hold her, let her play with your fingers. She will find them fascinating to watch. They are also great objects for her to practice reaching for, grabbing, and putting in her mouth because when she lets go, they are still there. Happily, they won't fall to the floor, the way her other toys do.

Day 117

You can never tell your baby too often how much you love him. Here is a fun song to let him know you love him all day long.

Skinnamarinka dinka dink
Skinnamarinka doo
I love you (I love you)

Skinnamarinka dinka dink
Skinnamarinka dinka doo
I love you (I love you)

I love you in the morning
And in the afternoon
I love you in the evening
Underneath the moon

Oh, skinnamarinka dinka dink
Skinnamarinka doo
I love you
I love you (whisper)

Day 118

Give your baby some new exercises to do. Make it more fun by doing them to music. Remember to do them slowly and gently.

1. Hold your baby's hands and bring his arms close to his sides, then stretch his arms overhead. Repeat several times.

2. Hold your baby's lower legs and bicycle his legs by bending one knee, while lowering the other.

Day 119

When you talk to your baby, vary your speech patterns. Be expressive! Use both a high voice and a low voice when you speak to her. You are instinctively teaching your baby to recognize the tone and rhythm of her native language.

Reflections on the Week

Teach us to number our days and recognize how few they are; help us to spend them as we should.

PSALM 90:12 TLB

This is the day the LORD has made; let us rejoice and be glad in it.

PSALM 118:24

Cherish the Moment

Your baby is getting older; she has lost that newborn look. Each day she is growing bigger, stronger, and smarter. She is now so much more in tune with what is going on around her. Take the time to cherish every precious moment with her before these moments slip away. When you lay her down to sleep, it's tempting to quickly rush off and get something accomplished. Instead, take the time to cuddle your baby, gaze at that beautiful face, kiss her plump cheeks, and stroke her perfect little hands. Two years from now you will lament over how quickly these days have passed!

We all need to be careful not to rush through our days and miss the pleasures that each one brings. Sometimes it is easy to think, "I can't wait until she can feed herself or entertain herself or _____ (you fill in the blank), so I can get something done." Don't be in a hurry for her to grow up. If you always live anticipating the day to come, you may miss out on the blessings this day can bring. Savor each day and cherish each experience because before long she won't be a baby anymore.

*D*ear God, I love being a mother! I love being with my baby. Sometimes though, it is easy to reflect on my carefree days before I had a child. I pretty much only had to worry about myself. Help me not to long for the past or anxiously await the future, but instead enjoy every phase of my child's life. Please help me not to let a single moment slip away unappreciated. I want to enjoy each moment I have with my baby. Amen.

Week 18

Day 120

Lay your baby on his tummy. Put your hands against the soles of his feet. He will push off your hands and inch forward. Let him continue pushing off your hands to get the feeling of propelling himself forward.

Your Baby Is
Four Months Old!

Day 121

When you take a picture of your baby, jot it down on your calendar and note what she was wearing. Now when you get around to having your film developed, you can remember exactly how old she was. If your camera has a date function, you can use this instead.

It's time for your baby's
four-month checkup.

Day 122

Tone up your body with your baby's help. Lie on the floor with your feet on the sofa. Place your baby, sitting up, on your tummy and hold him. Tilt your pelvis and lift your hips, giving your baby a ride up. Now lower your hips to give him a ride down.

Day 123

You should have received your baby's birth certificate and social security card by now. Write her social security number down and keep it someplace in your wallet for easy reference. Often doctors, insurance companies, and schools will need this information. Make several copies of her birth certificate before putting it and the social security card in a safe deposit box or other secure place. This will save you time in the future when you need to show copies for school and sports participation.

Day 124

Play "airplane" with your baby. Fly him slowly through the air in front of you with your hands securely around his waist. He will enjoy the flying sensation and it will strengthen his neck and back.

Day 125

Let your baby spend ten minutes, once or twice a day, playing by himself in a playpen with a few toys. Pick a time when he is happy and alert. Using the playpen will help your baby learn to entertain himself and will provide a safe place for him when you are busy. It is a good idea to let your baby get used to a playpen now, before he is mobile. When he does begin to crawl and roll around, he will just accept the playpen as part of his playtime instead of seeing it as a restriction.

Day 126

Lay your baby on her tummy and stack a few soft blocks in front of her. Let her knock over the blocks. Clap for her and say, "All fall down!" She will love watching them fall. Any time your baby spends on her stomach, even if it's just for a couple of minutes, develops the upper body strength and coordination necessary for important motor development.

Reflections on the Week

Do everything without complaining or arguing, so that you may become blameless and pure, children of God.

PHILIPPIANS 2:14-15

Whatever you do, work at it with all your heart, as working for the Lord, not for men, since you know that you will receive an inheritance from the Lord as a reward. It is the Lord Christ you are serving.

COLOSSIANS 3:23-24

Oh, Those Endless Chores

Let's face it, much of what mothers do can be repetitive and monotonous. There never seems to be a beginning or an end to this job. Even when you get something completed, it doesn't stay that way for long. As soon as you put away the last piece of laundry, there is already something new to be washed in the laundry basket. As soon as the dishes and kitchen are cleaned up, it's soon time to prepare the next meal. The same is true for wiping noses, changing diapers, and cleaning house. It can be easy to get bogged down in what seems like one long, mindless series of chores.

Your attitude toward these chores will either cause you to feel like an underpaid maid or free you to see a greater purpose in them so you can do your job without resentment. You have a choice regarding what your attitude will be. Let me encourage you to view your service to your family as an offering to God, an act of service to Him. Giving of yourself to help others honors God.

I love this principle: If we do each of our tasks with the mind-set that we are doing it for God, we can put love into everything we do. By doing this, we are setting a great example for our children. Do they see us grumbling and complaining as we go about our days? Is there a "woe is me" attitude? Will our children grow up feeling they are a burden instead of a blessing? We need to think of our chores as a way to bless our families by making our homes a pleasant place for them to be. When we clean, we can thank God that we have been blessed with all these things to clean. As we fold each family member's clean laundry, we can take the time to pray for that person. Remember, cooking and cleaning is not our main job anyway; loving, teaching, and encouraging our children is what is truly important.

Dear Lord, it is so easy to get discouraged by the number of mindless tasks I need to do repeatedly every day. I confess I often feel resentful about it. Please help change my perspective. Help me to see these tasks as a way I can bless my family as I care for them. Help me see my work as an act of service to You. God, I am thankful that You have given me this home to clean, this baby to care for, and this food to prepare. You are so very good to me! Amen.

Week 19

Day 127

Your baby will enjoy the "conversation" between your hands as you sing, "Where is Thumbkin?" to him. He will begin to look back and forth as each hand moves.

Where is Thumbkin?	*(hands behind back)*
Where is Thumbkin?	*(hands behind back)*
Here I am!	*(put your right thumb in front of you and bend it to "talk")*
Here I am!	*(put your left thumb in front of you and bend it to "talk")*
How are you today, sir?	*(bend your right thumb to "talk")*
Very well, I thank you	*(bend your left thumb to "talk")*
Run away	*(put your right hand behind your back)*
Run away	*(put your left hand behind your back)*

Continue with Pointer, Tall Man, Ring Man, Pinkie, and All the Men.

Day 128

Keep a large plastic storage box under the crib. As your baby outgrows an outfit, wash it, button/snap it, and put it in the box. When the box is full, label it, "Outgrew by _____ months." Start a new box for the next set of outgrown clothes. The clothes will be all ready to save for your next baby, to donate, or to sell at a garage sale. Your baby's clothes will always be organized with very little effort.

Day 129

Give your baby an elevator ride. Lie on your back with your baby resting on your torso. Hold her firmly around her chest and lift her slowly overhead. This is not only fun, but also strengthens her neck and back while strengthening your arms and chest. Just watch out for that drool!

Day 130

Sit your baby on your lap facing you and sing, "Pop! Goes the Weasel."

> *All around the mulberry bush*
> *The monkey chased the weasel*
> *The monkey thought it was all in fun*
> *Then pop goes the weasel!*
> *(bounce him up on your knees)*

Day 131

Although it is not necessary to clean your baby's toys all the time, it is a good idea to clean them periodically, especially as she starts putting them in her mouth more. An easy way to wash and disinfect many toys at once is to put them in the top rack of your dishwasher and run them through a dishwashing cycle. Bath toys can be washed with a little bleach in the washing machine to remove any mold or mildew.

Day 132

When you make a recipe that freezes well, double or triple the recipe. This won't take you any more time to prepare, but it will allow you to make several meals at once. Label, date, and freeze the extra portions. Now when you have a day where you are too busy or tired to cook, you have an easy homemade meal ready to heat up.

Day 133

Wipe your baby's gums with a damp washcloth before bedtime to clean them. Getting her used to this routine now will make brushing her teeth less of a battle in the future.

Reflections on the Week

Our mouths were filled with laughter, our tongues with songs of joy.

PSALM 126:2

Sarah said, "God has brought me laughter, and everyone who hears about this will laugh with me."

GENESIS 21:6

The Sounds of Laughter

When was the last time you had a really good belly laugh? It feels good all over to laugh! Laughter will relieve some of the tension in your life. Don't let the responsibilities of mothering outweigh the joys. A sense of humor will help you get through each day. When you can relax and laugh at your situation or yourself, it helps put things into proper perspective. When you choose to see the funny side of a situation, it diffuses much of the frustration and stress. Laughter truly is the best medicine, and it softens the rough edges in relationships.

Children need to see grownups laughing and having fun. Isn't it great there is so much in life to laugh about? Look for it; find something to laugh about. Laugh long and hard until the tears run down your face. That laughter will echo through the walls of your home for a long time to come. What a wonderful gift to be able to pass on to your children!

Dear Lord, let there always be laughter ringing through the walls of our home. I love to hear my baby laugh. It is one of my favorite sounds in the whole world. Let laughter be a regular occurrence in our family. When things don't go as planned, help me learn to laugh about it instead of becoming frustrated. Help me to find joy and humor in whatever situations arise during the day. Amen.

Week 20

Day 134

Play a musical instrument for your baby (harmonica, guitar, piano, or anything else you may have). He will be intrigued with watching how you are able to make music come out of an object.

Day 135

Sing this finger-play song to your baby:

Open, shut them, open, shut them	*(open and close hands to a fist)*
Give a little clap	*(clap)*
Open, shut them, open, shut them	*(open and close hands to a fist)*
Fold them in your lap	*(put them in your lap)*
Creep them, creep them, slowly creep them	*(walk fingers up his tummy)*
Right up to your chin	*(tickle under his chin)*
Open wide your little mouth	*(touch his mouth)*
But do not let them in!	*(run fingers down his tummy)*

Day 136

Life may seem incredibly busy, but what else can you expect when you have such an important job? What you are doing now—building a loving relationship, nurturing your child's development, modeling compassion, and instilling godly values—affects not only your child, but eventually the world as well, as you influence the next generation.

Day 137

Your baby doesn't need to wear shoes until she begins to walk, but most babies have their first pair of shoes much earlier. Usually you or a friend just couldn't resist buying a pair of those tiny adorable shoes. When she outgrows them, they probably won't be very worn, so stitch or glue a ribbon to them and make a memorable Christmas ornament to cherish for years to come. This could also be the beginning of a family tradition where you make or purchase a Christmas ornament each year that reflects an interest your child has. Each year place the date on the new ornament. When she is an adult and has moved into her own home, you can give the collection to her as a special gift.

Day 138

Sing and hold up your fingers as you say the numbers. This is also a fun song to sing as you go up the stairs.

1, 2 buckle my shoe

3, 4 shut the door

5, 6 pick up sticks

7, 8 lay them straight

9, 10 a big fat hen (in a deep voice)

Day 139

Hold your baby facing outward in front of a mirror. Hold one of your arms between his legs, with the other around his waist. Say:

> *Ticktock, ticktock (rock side to side)*
> *Cuckoo, cuckoo (lean forward two times)*

Your baby will love the anticipation of the "cuckoo"!

Day 140

It is never too early to start instilling God's Word in your baby's life. As you open the curtains in the morning, say, "This is the day the Lord has made; let us rejoice and be glad in it" (Psalm 118:24).

Reflections on the Week

Then, because so many people were coming and going that they did not even have a chance to eat, he said to them,

"Come with me by yourselves to a quiet place and get some rest."

MARK 6:31

By the seventh day God had finished the work he had been doing; so on the seventh day he rested from all his work.

GENESIS 2:2

Take Time for Yourself

It may sometimes seem as though your job as a mother never ends. There are no coffee breaks, lunch breaks, or weekends off. You are on duty 24 hours a day, seven days a week, 365 days a year. There is never any down time; you are always taking care of something or someone. It is easy to get lost in the constant demand on your time, energy, and body. It is important for you to take care of yourself to prevent feeling burned out and short-tempered.

When God set aside the seventh day as a day of rest, He knew that we all need to take a break from our work. When we rest, it benefits not only ourselves but those around us as well. When we put aside our own needs for rest and relaxation, we become grouchy, quick-tempered, impatient, and less loving—not much fun to be around! When we begin to feel resentful of the time our babies demand from us, that is usually a good sign that we are in need of some rest and refreshment.

Carve out time daily for yourself, even if it's just ten or fifteen minutes. Be on the lookout for free pockets of time, and don't feel guilty claiming them as your own. At naptime, turn off the ringer on the phone, put a sign over the doorbell that says everyone is napping, and forget about your to-do list. Do something that relaxes or replenishes you. Call a friend, flip through a magazine, take a nap, work in your garden, or start a craft project. Sometimes we need to take time just to be quiet and alone without doing anything.

Keep growing as a person. Learn something new; challenge your mind. Let your husband have the opportunity to bond with your baby and take an evening or Saturday morning off to go out with friends, pursue a hobby, or take a class. You are in this for the long haul. Be careful that in your zeal to be a good mother, you don't burn yourself out at the beginning.

Dear God, thank You for teaching me the principle of rest in Your Word. Motherhood seems to require my giving 100 percent of myself all the time. I am beginning to realize that I need to carve some time out for myself so I can come back to my job as a mother rested, restored, and refreshed. Help me not to wait until my well has run empty, but instead regularly replenish myself so I can be the best possible mom. Amen.

Week 21

Day 141

Bring your baby outside to enjoy the outdoors. Lay him on a blanket under a tree and let him watch the leaves blow and hear them rustle. Let him reach out and touch the grass.

Day 142

When you play with your baby, sit her on the floor between your straddled legs with her back against your tummy. This will help her learn to sit up by strengthening her muscles.

Day 143

A happy, positive spirit can be nurtured in your baby early on. Look in a mirror with your baby. When she smiles at her reflection, point to her mouth and say, "Look, there's _____'s smile!" If she's not smiling say, "Where's your smile?" in a playful tone and then tickle her gently. As she smiles say, "There's that pretty smile God gave you!"

Day 144

Sing this song as your baby kicks his feet. Sing to the tune of "Row, Row, Row Your Boat."

One, two, three, four, five
Kick your little feet
Six, seven, eight, nine, ten
In your baby seat

Day 145

Help your baby learn to roll over. Kneel on one side of her as she lays on her back and very gently pull her far leg over toward you so that she starts to roll on her tummy. Help the rest of her body to follow her leg, to finish rolling over.

Day 146

Give your baby a tummy massage. Lay your hands flat over the center of her chest. Slide your hands out to her sides, and then bring them down toward her belly button. This is the same movement you would use if you were smoothing a wrinkle out of a sheet.

Day 147

Put a bib on your baby when you first start feeding him solid foods. He will learn that this is nonnegotiable and part of the eating routine. As a result, he won't resist a bib later when he will really need to use one.

Reflections on the Week

Every good and perfect gift is from above, coming down from the Father of the heavenly lights.

JAMES 1:17

Praise the LORD. How good it is to sing praises to our God, how pleasant and fitting to praise him!

PSALM 147:1

I Love Being a Mom!

Isn't being a mom great? A powerful bond has formed between our babies and ourselves. Our hearts simply overflow with love for them. They are so engaging as we play with them, so endearing as they smile at us, so enamoring as they sleep peacefully in our arms. Their contagious giggles brighten our day. Not a moment goes by when we aren't thinking about them. Mother love is a love like no other.

God has picked out the best children for you and me. He has a special plan for each one. Every day our babies are growing, changing, and learning something new. We are beginning to see traits from both sides of the family coming out in their personalities and appearances. It is exciting to see who God has created our children to grow up to be!

Dear God, I love being a mom! Thank You for the privilege of mothering this child. Thank You, Lord, for the increased confidence You have given me in mothering (although there is still so much I don't know). Today was a good day. I thank You for days like these! May I always appreciate all I have. I praise You for all You have given me, especially this precious child. Amen.

Week 22

Day 148

Play with your baby's feet in different ways. Rub them
together, wiggle each toe, clap them together, gently
rotate her feet at the ankle, and touch her toes to her
chin. It's amazing how flexible babies are!

Day 149

Sit your baby on your lap. Put his hand on your
mouth as you talk to him and make funny sounds. He will
enjoy feeling your lips and jaw move. He is learning expe-
rientially how you use your lips and tongue to form
words.

Day 150

Your baby is starting to reach out and grab everything
she sees. Give her a wide variety of objects to hold to satisfy her curiosity and to help her practice moving her
hand towards an object. Don't give her too many toys at
once, though, or she will be overwhelmed. When you set
her down, always look carefully around the floor to make

sure there is nothing little she could pick up and put in her mouth.

Your Baby Is Five Months Old!

Day 151

Go out on a clear night and show her the moon and the stars. Sing, "Twinkle, Twinkle, Little Star" or say the poem, "I See the Moon."

I see the moon and the moon sees me.
God bless the moon and God bless me.

Day 152

Here's a tip to make feeding your baby less messy. When you spoon out the baby food, wipe the bottom of the spoon off on the bowl. Feed your baby a spoonful, and then wipe the spoon sideways across her mouth to scrape off the excess from her face.

Day 153

Getting to church with your baby can be a major undertaking, but try to remember the big picture. You are showing by your actions the importance of going to church to worship, praise, and learn about God. Prepare as much as you can on Saturday night to make Sunday morning less stressful. Lay out everyone's clothes, pack the diaper bag, have the breakfast dishes set out, find everyone's shoes and coats, and so on. Let Sundays be a wonderful experience for your baby, not one of short tempers and glaring looks.

Day 154

Sing this song to the tune of "Mary Had a Little Lamb" while touching your fingers to your baby's toes.

Touch your fingers to your toes

To your toes, to your toes

Touch your fingers to your toes

1, 2, 3, 4, 5   *(count each toe)*

Reflections on the Week

Be careful, and watch yourselves closely so that you do not forget the things your

*eyes have seen or let them slip from your
heart as long as you live. Teach them to
your children and to their children after
them.*

DEUTERONOMY 4:9

*Each of you is to take up a stone...to
serve as a sign among you. In the future,
when your children ask you, "What do
these stones mean?" tell them that...
these stones are to be a memorial to the
people of Israel forever."*

JOSHUA 4:5-7

Creating Memories

One of the fun parts of your job as a mother is to be
the family historian. The moments you record in photos
and words will be the ones most remembered by your
children and by you. Your children rely on you to be their
early memory. You will be amazed at how quickly you will
forget all the precious things your child is doing now.
Take the time to record the things they do and say to prevent this memory loss later. Of course, you can't capture
every moment on film. Sometimes you need to just sit
back and enjoy the moment, simply treasuring the
memory in your heart.

Throughout the pages of this book are many ideas on
how to record memories. Try to incorporate as many as
you can. Believe me, it will be time well spent. Photos,
letters, journals, baby books, and videos will be looked at

again and again. Not just by you, but by your child as she gets older. These stored memories will be a blessing to her as she reflects on the happy memories you have built together.

Begin creating your own family traditions, merging the best from both your husband's and your family together. These traditions don't have to center only around holidays. Look for ways to make your everyday life special. Have a special way to say goodnight to each other, to celebrate each other's successes, and to signal "I love you" from a distance. You are creating memories that you and your child will carry for a lifetime, memories that make up the tapestry of life.

Dear Lord, my baby is changing so quickly and learning to do so many new things. I don't want to forget any of it. Help me do a good job of recording her first year so we can enjoy looking at it when she's older. Please help me build positive memories in the life of my child so we will have many happy moments to look back on in the future. Amen.

Week 23

Day 155

Fill your cheeks up with air. Use your baby's hands to "pop" your cheeks. He will love watching your face change and hearing the "pop" sound. Older siblings will love doing this with their baby brother or sister.

Day 156

Don't let your house become too cluttered. Pick up things as you go along. Your baby will begin to learn to pick up when she is finished, before starting something new. Babies love order, even if it is just so they can enjoy making it disorderly again!

Day 157

You've probably noticed that your baby loves to watch other children. No one can entertain her in quite the same way nor make her laugh quite so hard. If your baby doesn't have any siblings, invite someone over to visit who has young children. Another opportunity to watch older children is to bring her to the park so she can watch them play.

Day 158

When your baby is taking his bath, pour a thin stream of water on his hands. He will enjoy feeling the water run over his fingers. He might even try to grab it. Tell him how good God is to give us water to drink and to keep us clean.

Day 159

Your baby will be undeniably messy when he eats, but you can keep it somewhat under control. Start by holding the jar of food instead of setting it on the high chair tray where he can reach it. Teach him not to put his hands in his mouth as you feed him, otherwise it will end up all over his face and hair. He may look cute now, but think long term. Are you going to want to wash his hair after every meal? When he innocently goes to put his hands in his mouth, just gently guide his hands down to the tray and say, "Let's keep our hands on the tray." Soon enough he will have the opportunity to use his hands to eat when he graduates to finger foods.

Day 160

Bring your baby to a pet store. She will love watching all the animals move and hearing the different sounds they make.

Day 161

Let your baby stand on your lap as you hold his torso. He will think he is pretty hot stuff to be able to stand! As he gets stronger, just hold him by the hands.

Reflections on the Week

[Martha] had a sister called Mary, who sat at the Lord's feet listening to what he said. But Martha was distracted by all the preparations that had to be made. She came to him and asked, "Lord, don't you care that my sister has left me to do the work by myself? Tell her to help me!" "Martha, Martha," the Lord answered, "you are worried and upset about many things, but only one thing is needed. Mary has chosen what is better, and it will not be taken away from her."

LUKE 10:39-42

Now this is what the LORD Almighty says: "Give careful thought to your ways."

HAGGAI 1:5

Have Realistic Expectations

Are you a doer, perhaps an overachiever? Are you like Martha in the Bible who was always busy getting things done? I can certainly relate to her! As a new mother, however, you have to lower your expectations of what you can realistically get done in a day. This is not the time in your life when you should be trying to accomplish many things. You will miss out on enjoying your baby if you are always trying to complete a project or are thinking about what needs to be done next. When you set unrealistic expectations for yourself, it robs you of the joy you could be experiencing. You don't have to give up everything; but just be a little more realistic in what you can handle. For example, maybe you had hopes of planting a garden this year, but realistically in this season of life, all you may be able to do is plant a pot of flowers to set by the front door. You have many years ahead of you to complete all the things you want to do.

Completing tasks gives us all a sense of accomplishment and make us feel good about ourselves, but our value is not measured by what we accomplish. God's love for us isn't dependent on how many things we check off our lists today. He loves us because we are His, and nothing we do can make Him love us any more!

Dear Lord, I was so used to being efficient and getting everything done before I became a mother. Now I feel as though I never get anything done. Help me to set realistic expectations. Remind me that my worth is not based on how much I accomplish. I know I can't be an effective mother when there are too many other things competing for my attention. Raising a child is a full-time job in itself. Help me to be more like Mary, who focused on what was important, and less like Martha, who was preoccupied with her to-do list. Amen.

Week 24

Day 162

Don't let a single moment slip away unsavored or unappreciated. These days are priceless. Enjoy every phase, every stage. Don't wish away your baby's childhood by saying "If only he were talking, if only he were walking…" Motherhood should not be a burden, but a joy and a blessing. Live so you can look back on these years with no regrets.

Day 163

Sing this song to remind your baby how much Jesus loves her.

1 - 2 - 3	*(count with fingers)*
Jesus loves me	*(point to self)*
1 - 2	*(count with fingers)*
Jesus loves you	*(point to your baby)*
3 and 4	*(count with fingers)*
He loves you more	*(point to your baby)*
More than you've ever been loved before	*(clap to beat)*
Oh, 1 - 2 - 3	*(count with fingers)*
Jesus loves me	*(point to self)*
1 - 2	*(count with fingers)*
Jesus loves you!	*(point to baby)*

Day 164

Help your baby to sit in front of a mirror by placing him between your legs. He can practice sitting up, and you can still see each other's faces. Let him put his hands on the mirror to touch his reflection.

Day 165

Sing, "Old MacDonald Had a Farm" with your baby. Don't be surprised if one of her first "words" is E-I-E-I-O.

Day 166

Praise your baby as he learns new things and masters new skills with lots of hugs, kisses, smiles, and encouraging words. You are his biggest cheerleader!

Day 167

Your baby can learn to thank God for her food from the first time she eats in the high chair. Pray before you set the food out, otherwise it will be too tempting for her to start eating. Hold your baby's hands together and say a simple prayer, such as, "Thank You, Jesus, for this food. Amen."

Day 168

Your baby will enjoy making noise and listening to the sounds different objects make. Give him the opportunity to experiment with different sounds—a wooden spoon and a pot to drum together, metal spoons to clink together, wooden blocks to bang, paper to crunch, a rattle to shake, or a toy that plays music.

Reflections on the Week

Our children too shall serve him, for they shall hear from us about the wonders of the Lord; generations yet unborn shall hear of all the miracles he did for us.

PSALM 22:30-31 TLB

From infancy you have known the holy Scriptures, which are able to make you wise for salvation through Jesus Christ.

2 TIMOTHY 3:15

Raising Your Children to Know God

One of your greatest responsibilities as a parent is to raise your children to know God. Don't wait until they are in grade school or even in preschool. Godly training can begin from the day your baby is born. So much of what children learn is caught, not taught, and this is true of their faith too. As you pray with your baby daily, he will see a habit of prayer interwoven into his daily life. Prayer will become second nature to him in the same way reading from a simple children's picture Bible or from Christian storybooks will lead to a familiarity with God's Word. Sing children's Bible songs and make up fun hand motions. Your love for God will shine brightly to your children.

Talk about God's goodness, His creation, and His love as you go about your day. Look for teachable moments to impart spiritual truth, then seize the moment. Make God a part of your everyday experiences as you pray for those in need when you hear a siren, or thank Him for a close parking spot, or admire how beautiful He made the world with all different kinds of flowers. As mothers, we have to train our minds to look for those moments and then use them to teach our children. We are the stewards of our children's souls as we prepare the next generation to love and serve God.

Dear Heavenly Father, I want to raise my child to know You, to love You, and to serve You. Help me to know how best to do that. Let my relationship with You overflow to my child. I know my child's perception of You will be affected by what kind of parent I am. Please help me to be loving, kind, and quick to forgive so that as he gets older, it will be easy for him to grasp the concept of a loving God. Let me be a reflection of You to my child. Amen.

Week 25

Day 169

Prop your baby in a sitting position with pillows. Sit across from her and hold a toy up in the air in front of her. Drop the toy and say, "Down it goes." Let her watch several times, then hand her the toy. See if she can drop the toy. It is harder than it looks. It takes practice and a lot of coordination to be able to consciously let go of something.

Day 170

Lay your baby on his tummy. Put a ribbon on the ground in front of him and wiggle it. Let him play with it, then move it slightly out of his reach. Let him reach and wriggle to grasp it. This will encourage him to reach and move forward.

Day 171

An inexpensive way to keep your floor clean under the high chair is to buy 1½ yards of clear (12 gauge) vinyl from a fabric store. Cut it to the size you need, and you have the perfect splat mat. You can also cut a piece to put under your baby's car seat to protect your car upholstery from spills.

Day 172

Sing "Two Little Blackbirds" to your baby.

Two little blackbirds sitting on a hill	*(put your pointer fingers up next to each other)*
One named Jack	*(wiggle your right pointer finger)*
And one named Jill	*(wiggle your left pointer finger)*
Fly away Jack	*(put your right hand behind your back)*
Fly away Jill	*(put your left hand behind your back)*
Come back Jack	*(bring your right hand out in front again)*
Come back Jill	*(bring your left hand out in front again)*

Day 173

The older your baby gets, the more social she will become. Help her learn to wave goodbye to people. When you pass by your baby, wave to her. It won't be long before she will be able to wave back at you.

Day 174

Your baby is becoming more aware of his feet. Lift his legs up so he can see his two little feet. Help him discover ways to play with this great new toy by helping him grab on to his feet. You can also play "This Little Piggy."

This little piggy went to market	*(wiggle his big toe)*
This little piggy stayed home	*(wiggle second toe)*
This little piggy ate roast beef	*(wiggle third toe)*
This little piggy had none	*(wiggle fourth toe)*
And this little piggy went "Wee, wee, wee," all the way home	*(wiggle pinky toe)*

Day 175

When your baby can't see you, keep in touch with her through your voice. You could say from the kitchen, "_____, Mommy's washing the dishes. I'll be done in a minute." She will learn that you are present even when she can't see you. This is true of her heavenly Father also.

Reflections on the Week

I praise you because [my baby] is fearfully and wonderfully made; your works are wonderful, I know that full well.

PSALM 139:14

My brothers, as believers in our glorious
Lord Jesus Christ, don't show favoritism.

JAMES 2:1

No Comparisons Allowed

Have you ever been with a group of moms when the
conversation turns to what developmental milestones
each baby has accomplished? Do you ever feel a sting of
envy that your baby is not doing what your friend's child
is doing? Or do you get a smug feeling that your child is
way ahead of his age developmentally?

Babies master each new skill when they are developmentally ready. No two children are alike. They each
grow and learn in their own way and at their own pace
based on their personality, disposition, and activity level.
An active baby may be developing her large motor skills,
while a quieter baby might be fine-tuning her eye-hand
coordination. In the end, your baby will learn how to do it
all, and you will be able to fill in all those blank spaces in
her baby book. If you have serious concerns about your
baby's development, speak with your pediatrician, but in
most cases your baby will develop on her own timetable.

Maybe your baby always seems serious and subdued
while your friend's baby is friendly and happy. Or perhaps
your baby is a loud bundle of energy while your
neighbor's child is calm and quiet. You may wonder what
you are doing wrong. It's normal for mothers to compare
their babies with others to see how they measure up.
Keep in mind, however, that God creates each child
uniquely. Parenting is not a competition. Your child's

disposition will go through many changes as she develops. I have seen sweet, happy babies become belligerent three-year-olds, and shy, clingy two-year-olds become friendly, outgoing six-year-olds. Don't be too quick to label your child. Just encourage her strengths and help work on her weaknesses.

Dear Lord, help me not to compare my baby with others, but instead delight in her uniqueness. I know You created her in just the perfect way, and in Your time she will learn how to do all things. There are some areas of development where she seems to be ahead of other babies her age. Help me to be careful to never say anything that would make another mother feel her baby is not as advanced. As my baby's personality begins to blossom, help me be careful not to label her, but instead realize that she is a work in progress. Amen.

Week 26

Day 176

As your baby begins to babble, encourage him to talk by repeating back the sounds he makes, then pause to give him a chance to vocalize again. Turn his sounds into words for him, as they are precursors to real words.

Day 177

The next time your baby falls asleep in your arms, savor the moment. Listen to her rhythmic breathing, inhale her sweet scent, and feel her small body snuggled against yours. Do not rush off, but linger a little longer. Store this moment in your memory to cherish forever!

Day 178

If you are behind on your baby book, try to catch up now before it all becomes a blur. Try to update it each month so it does not become an overwhelming task. This book will become one of your and your baby's most valuable possessions.

Day 179

Turn on some upbeat music and have fun dancing your baby around the room, swinging, dipping, and twirling.

Day 180

Read books to your baby in different ways. Sometimes read the text so she gets used to listening to a story. Other times point to the pictures and talk about what you see, naming things. When you point, do it from the left side of the page to the right. This begins to train her eyes to read from left to right.

Day 181

Sing "If You're Happy and You Know It" and help your baby do the movements to the different verses.

If you're happy and you know it, clap your hands	*(clap his hands)*
If you're happy and you know it, clap your hands	*(clap his hands)*
If you're happy and you know it, then your face will surely show it	
If you're happy and you know it, clap your hands!	*(clap his hands)*

2. Stomp your feet   *(move his feet up and down)*

3. Shout hurrah!   *(move his fist up in the air)*

4. Do all three   *(do all three motions in a row)*

Your Baby Is Six Months Old!

Day 182

When you are outside, talk about God and the beauty of His creation. Say, "Look at the beautiful flowers God made," or "God makes the wind blow to cool us off," or "God is a wonderful artist. Look at the beautiful sunset He painted for us." It may feel funny at first, but it will help God's name to become a natural part of your baby's vocabulary. It will also help you get in the habit of teaching your child about God as you go about your day.

Reflections on the Week

For God is not a God of disorder, but of peace.

1 CORINTHIANS 14:33

The wise heart will know the proper time and procedure. For there is a proper time and procedure for every matter.

ECCLESIASTES 8:5-6

Getting Organized

Time. There never seems to be enough of it to get everything done. Who would have thought a little baby could take up so much time? Managing your home, however, is a crucial part of being an effective mother. As you learn the skills of housekeeping and home management, you will become more organized, save time, and have a peaceful home. Here are some more tips to help you run your home efficiently.

Calendar—Keep a monthly calendar where both you and your husband write down any necessary dates as soon as you know them. In addition, keep a weekly calendar for yourself. Mine is divided into hourly slots so I can better schedule my day. Write everything down you need to do so you don't have to try and remember it all in your head. On your weekly calendar, keep a to-do list, a to-call list, and an errand list. When you have a free moment, you can get one of the things done on your list and then enjoy the satisfaction of checking it off. Try to run all your errands in one day. Look at your weekly planner each evening so you know where you need to be and what must be done the following day. This will help you to be better prepared for tomorrow.

Paper—Paper can sometimes seem to take over our life. Purchase an expandable file and label the sections, "Bills to Pay," "Correspondence—Reply Needed," and "Information for Upcoming Events." When you go through the mail, toss all junk mail and unnecessary pieces. Place other mail in the relevant file sections. File your statements and bills into a file cabinet as soon as you have paid them. Don't save entire magazines—just tear out the articles or ideas you want to save and file them by topic for future reference.

Grocery Shopping—Make up a preprinted grocery list that has a blank section for each aisle of your favorite store. Write headings over each section as to the main items in each aisle. This takes a little time to make, but will save you a lot of time on every shopping trip. Write down items as you need them on your grocery list in the correct space. Also note any advertised items that are on sale you may want to buy. On the night before you shop, decide on the next week's menu and list all the ingredients you will need. With your organized list, you can move quickly up and down the aisles and will only have to grocery shop once a week.

Dear Lord, help me to be more organized so I can manage my home well. Let me make good use of my time by streamlining my efforts and planning ahead. Help me have an orderly, peaceful home. Even though much of my housework goes unnoticed and unappreciated, thank You that You see all that I do and will not forget my work. Please help me to have a joyful, thankful heart as I go about my day. Amen.

The Third
Three Months

A Bundle of Baby Babbling

One little tongue to speak His truth,
One little heart for Him in youth,
Take them, O Jesus, let them be
Always willing, true to Thee.

AUTHOR UNKNOWN

Week 27

Day 183

An important skill for your baby to develop is the ability to entertain herself. Give her opportunities to play on her own so she can learn to do this. It will help her become more creative and prevent her from becoming easily bored.

Day 184

It's time to record your baby's voice on your audiotape again. Add it to the recording you did at three months. Try to get him laughing on tape so you can remember that wonderful baby laugh.

It's time for your baby's
six-month checkup.

Day 185

Lay your baby on her tummy and place a small pillow under her chest for support. This will put her in a more comfortable position to use her hands to play with her toys.

Day 186

Wear a hooded sweatshirt with drawstrings. Lean over your baby as he is lying down. He will love to catch the strings and pull on them. This is a great way for him to develop his fine motor skills. He will also love being able to look at your face close to his as he plays.

Day 187

Leave your camera out in an easily accessible place so you are able to catch special moments on film. You will end up getting pictures that capture more of her personality than if you just pull out your camera every once in a while and have her pose. Also be sure to get plenty of everyday moments on videotape. Videotape her as she is waking up and first sees your face, as you rock and sing her a lullaby, or as you play with her on the floor. Both of you will love looking back at this as she gets older.

Day 188

When your baby is making sounds, gently pat his mouth quickly with your hand. He will enjoy the funny new sound he can make.

Day 189

Sing this song to your baby. Soon she will be able to clap along with you!

Clap your hands	*(clap your hands)*
1 - 2 - 3	*(count with your fingers)*
Clap your hands	*(clap your hands)*
Just like me	*(point to yourself)*
Tell your hands to go away	*(put your hands behind your back)*
Find your hands so we can play	*(bring your hands back out in front again)*

Reflections on the Week

Dear children, let us not love with words or tongue but with actions and in truth.

1 JOHN 3:18

May the Lord make your love increase and overflow for each other and for everyone else.

1 THESSALONIANS 3:12

Loving Your Baby

Love is the most important ingredient in parenting. The love for our babies is so deep, so steadfast, and so pure it can take our breath away. Fortunately, our children don't have to earn our love; we shower it upon them freely, sacrificially. It grows from the closeness that we establish through snuggling, playing, talking, and spending time with them. Let God's love flow out of you.

Your children's lives are shaped by your love. Even though you feel the love for your children deep within your hearts, make sure you express it to them in a way they can comprehend—through your actions. Your baby will feel your love most clearly by your physical affection— cuddling, caressing, and tenderly holding him. I think God designed babies' soft bodies with this in mind. They are so irresistible to hold! When you spend time playing and interacting with your baby, you are demonstrating your love. As you become attuned to his needs and learn his likes and dislikes, you form an even closer bond of love and affection.

You will also communicate love to your child by what you say. Coo with him, sing to him, and tell him over and over how much you love him. Let him know how thankful you are that God gave him to you. Use affectionate nick- names—special names that are meant just for him. These terms of endearment will be a special way for you to say "I love you" throughout your child's life. Your baby may not understand all your words, but he can tell from your tone of voice, your eyes, and your facial expression that you are saying something special.

Dear Heavenly Father, I feel such an incredible love for my baby. Amazingly, You love him a million times more. Please, Lord, let my baby always feel secure in my love. Help me to express it in ways that he can understand. As he goes through difficult stages in his childhood, help my love to never waver. Amen.

Week 28

Day 190

Sing the alphabet song to your baby. Even though he won't know what letters are for a long time, anything that is put to music is easier to remember.

Day 191

Your baby is beginning to use the pincer grasp to pick up small objects. Let her use this skill and her natural curiosity to pick something out of your pocket. Let your baby watch you put a toy, closed pen, or piece of paper in your pocket. Make sure some of the object is still visible. Say, "Where is my pen?" Let her grab it and pull it out. Say, "You found it. You got my pen!" Your baby will love to do this over and over again.

Day 192

Sit your baby on your lap, facing you. Put your hands around his back. Lean him back slightly, then help him pull himself back up. Rock back and forth as you sing, "Row, Row, Row Your Boat." This is not only fun but will also strengthen his tummy muscles.

Row, row, row your boat
Gently down the stream
Merrily, merrily, merrily, merrily
Life is but a dream

Day 193

Give your baby a sponge and cup to play with in her bath. She will love filling and dumping the cup. She will also enjoy seeing the water drip out of the sponge as she squeezes it.

Day 194

Do this fun finger play with your baby.

The great big train goes up the track	*(walk your fingers up his tummy)*
It says "Toot, Toot"	*(tap his nose two times)*
Then it rolls right back	*(walk your fingers down his tummy)*

Day 195

Take several close-up pictures of your baby in a way that will be easy to duplicate (for example, lying on a blanket in diapers). Frame the best one. If you have another baby in the future, take the exact same picture of her at the same age and have the two pictures matted together in the same frame. If this is not your first baby, find a favorite picture of your first child at the same age and try to duplicate the location, clothing, and body position as best as you can with your new baby. Frame the pictures together.

Day 196

Let your baby try drinking from a sippy cup. Most babies love juice, so try using diluted juice to entice him to use a cup. A good time to practice using a cup is when he is in the bathtub with a cup of water. Even after he gets the hang of it, you will probably have to hold the cup for him for a while. Helping him become familiar with drinking from a cup will make weaning him from the bottle or breast easier.

Reflections for the Week

Do not worry about tomorrow, for tomorrow will worry about itself. Each day has enough trouble of its own.

MATTHEW 6:34

"For I know the plans I have for you," declares the LORD, "plans to prosper you and not to harm you, plans to give you hope and a future."

JEREMIAH 29:11

Leave Your Worries Behind

When you were waiting for your baby to arrive, you probably anticipated the intense love and pure delight you would feel when you saw him. But one emotion you probably didn't think about having when you became a mother was worry, even fear. With feelings of love also comes a feeling of protectiveness; the "mama bear" intuition kicks in. There seems to be so much to worry about—illness, injuries, accidents, kidnapping, SIDS. It's easy to worry about things that never concerned you before.

Fear and worry, however, aren't from God. Worry comes with a price; it can keep you from leading a peaceful life. Worry doesn't change or solve anything, and when you worry, you are not walking by faith. Of course, you need to be responsible to do all you can to keep your baby safe, but then you need to trust that God will protect him. He is in control, and He loves your child even more than you do.

We often spend time worrying about things that will never happen. When we become anxious, it not only affects us, but our children as well. Babies will pick up on our anxiety and may become fussy and fretful. Whenever we start to worry or become anxious, we should immediately turn our concerns over to God in prayer. It is then that we will feel a sense of peace, knowing that our loving God is in control.

Dear Lord, help me to have more faith so I am not filled with worry. You created this baby, and I know I can trust the details of his life with You. Help me to do all I can to keep him safe and secure and then leave the rest up to You. Amen.

Week 29

Day 197

Go easy on yourself; there is no such thing as a
perfect mother. It is okay to make a mistake. Your baby
hasn't read all the books. She probably doesn't have the
high expectations you put on yourself. Babies are very
forgiving. It will be quite awhile before she starts
comparing you with other mothers. Right now you are
her everything and she loves you!

Day 198

Your baby is beginning to understand what pointing
means. She realizes that when you point at something,
you are referring to that object. Take your baby for a walk
around the house and point at things as you talk about
them. Soon she will be pointing too!

Day 199

As you dress and undress your baby, name and touch
his body parts. The easiest ones to learn first seem to be
the eyes, nose, and mouth.

Day 200

Ask, "Can you give Mommy a kiss?" Then put your face right up to her mouth and say, "Oh, what a nice kiss!" Soon she will lean her head forward and give you a big kiss on her own. What could be better than that?

Day 201

As your baby begins to use his hands more, he can often be rough with them. Teach him what "be gentle" means. Stroke his face with your hand and say "gentle" in a soft voice. Hold his hand and help him stroke your face gently and say, "Oh, how gentle _____ is, so gentle with Mommy." Whenever he is rough, just take his hand and show him how to be gentle and say, "We need to be gentle."

Day 202

Do this finger play for your baby.

Here is the beehive	*(make a fist)*
Where are the bees?	*(with your other hand make a questioning motion)*
Hidden away where nobody sees	*(place your other hand over your fist)*
Soon they come creeping out of the hive	*(move your hand away from your fist)*

1 - 2 - 3 - 4 - 5	*(let your fingers pop out one at a time)*
Bzzz, bzzz!	*(fly your fingers over to tickle your baby)*

Day 203

Help your baby listen to and learn the names for everyday sounds. When you hear a sound (telephone, doorbell, siren, clock, or garage door opening), talk about it with her.

Reflections on the Week

> *Her husband has full confidence in her and lacks nothing of value. She brings him good, not harm, all the days of her life.*
>
> PROVERBS 31:11-12

> *Be patient with each other, making allowance for each other's faults because of your love.*
>
> EPHESIANS 4:2 TLB

Nurture Your Marriage Relationship

Take a moment to measure the pulse of your marriage relationship. Is it passionate and beating wildly?

Is it hanging in there, beating a little more slowly than before you and your spouse became parents? Are you having trouble picking up a heartbeat because life with your husband is a daily struggle? Whatever the heartbeat of your marriage is, it's important to realize you are setting the patterns now that will become patterns for the rest of your life. Your children need you to build a strong relationship with their father so their world will be secure and stable. You are not just partners in parenting; you are first husband and wife.

A marriage relationship needs tending, weeding, and nurturing just like a garden. Listen to one another's words, lean on each other's strengths, laugh together, be affectionate, pray together, focus on each other's good qualities, and make time to have fun together. Find ways to stay connected and foster a genuine intimacy. When you and your husband nurture your friendship, nothing you face together as a couple will seem too big to overcome.

When you go through difficult times, communicate openly and don't withdraw from each other. You are on the same team! Your strengths and weaknesses complement each other. Never even consider divorce as an option. Learn to disagree without being disagreeable, being as considerate to your husband as you would be with a friend.

Schedule date nights several times a month. Be creative as you have fun together. Your dates don't have to cost much money. Go on a hike, window-shop, get an ice cream cone, go bowling, play miniature golf, ride bikes, plan a picnic in the park, go back to where you had your first date, go to a roller skating or ice skating rink, or browse through a bookstore together.

If you can't find (or afford) a babysitter every week, plan some dates at home after your baby is asleep. Be creative. Here are some ideas to get you started: Stargaze in your backyard, rent a romantic movie, cook a meal together and eat by candlelight, play a board game, watch your wedding video, or look through old photo albums. What you decide to do is not what is important; it is the time you are spending together deepening your friendship that truly matters.

Dear Lord, I confess some days my husband gets put pretty low on my priority list. I don't intend to do it, but by the time he gets home, I am exhausted and preoccupied. Help me to find time for him. Please help me to better love him the way he is without trying to change him. Restore the fun and romance back into our relationship. Please bless our marriage, and thank You for this wonderful man You have put in my life. Amen.

Week 30

Day 204

Look at photos around your house with your baby. Point at and name the people in the pictures. This is especially good to do with photos of grandparents and other relatives he doesn't see often but whom you want him to remember.

Day 205

Baby proof your home now, before your baby is on the move. Put plastic plugs in all empty electrical outlets. Put child locks on doors of cabinets that store cleaning chemicals and other dangerous products. Bolt bookcases and any tall furniture to the wall that could tip over if she climbs or pulls up on them. Tie cords from window coverings up out of reach. Get down on your hands and knees and look around your house from a baby's perspective to see what other safety hazards there may be.

Day 206

Stand your baby next to the couch and let him lean against it. He may be able to stand there momentarily, supporting and balancing himself.

Day 207

When you lift up your baby, use the word "up" often. Say, "Up we go," or "Up to Mommy." This will help her understand the word and concept of "up."

Day 208

Tie a helium balloon to a long ribbon. Lay your baby on his back. Let him hold the ribbon and watch what happens as he pulls on it. This can keep him occupied for a long time, but you *must* stay right there with him as both the long ribbon and the balloon can be safety hazards. Deflate and throw out the balloon before it deflates on its own to eliminate any potential problems.

Day 209

Give your baby a basket filled with small toys. She will enjoy exploring the new treasures while she practices picking up and letting go of things.

Day 210

Help your baby learn words for his feelings—happy, sad, frustrated, excited, frightened, surprised. You could say, "Did that loud noise scare you?" or "I know, it made you sad when he pulled your toy away."

Reflections on the Week

Remain in me, and I will remain in you. No branch can bear fruit by itself; it must remain in the vine. Neither can you bear fruit unless you remain in me. I am the vine; you are the branches. If a man remains in me and I in him, he will bear much fruit; apart from me you can do nothing.

JOHN 15:4-5

God is our refuge and strength, an ever-present help in trouble...The LORD Almighty is with us.

PSALM 46:1,7

Depending Solely on God

Do you ever have days when you feel as though you just can't do it anymore? Do you have too many plates spinning, too many people who need you, too many responsibilities to meet, too much to do, and way too little time? Believe it or not, this is just the place where God can teach you the most. When you come to the point where you say, "I cannot possibly do this on my own. I need you, Lord," that is when God can move powerfully in your life.

None of us were created to be able to do it all on our own. God designed us to need Him to be able to live our lives, mother our children, and love our husbands. We often try relying on everything else—caffeine, friends, books, sheer determination—everything but the One who can fill us with wisdom, strength, patience, and self-control. When we are filled with God's presence, we have more to give to our families. His love naturally overflows out of our lives and into those around us. His peace will come over us as we deal with crying, needy children, and chaotic days. His wisdom will come to us as we make difficult decisions.

We need to surrender to God and become dependent on Him. He can then do great things through us. Things we can't even take credit for, like changed attitudes and new abilities that can only be attributed to His work in our lives.

*D*ear Lord, I thank You for Your presence in my life. I am sorry that I often place You in the backseat, while I try to stay in the driver's seat. Heavenly Father, while this task of mothering You gave me is wonderful, I just can't do it alone. It is too overwhelming. I step out in faith and ask You to come and be in the center of my life, where I can depend on You moment by moment. Help me to be the mother, wife, and woman of God You want me to be. Not so that I can take the credit, but so that You can be glorified. Amen.

Week 31

Day 211

Lay your baby on his back and hold one foot in each hand. Pedal his feet slowly then faster and faster as you say:

Motorboat, motorboat, go so slow
Motorboat, motorboat, go so fast
Motorboat, motorboat, step on the gas!

Day 212

If you will be traveling, don't forget to pack a night-light so your baby will not have to wake up in the dark. It will also prevent you from having to fumble through an unfamiliar place to check on her.

Your Baby Is
Seven Months Old!

Day 213

Let your baby sit with your family as you eat dinner. It might be more relaxing to feed him before you eat, but he can still join you to have a little snack. He will enjoy feeling part of the family conversation and seeing how you interact.

Day 214

You can begin to establish an early foundation for obedience now. Set him up for success by asking him only to do things that he would do anyway. Hand him a toy you know he can easily hold. Say, " _____, hold this toy, please." When he holds it, praise him for obeying you. Say, "Good boy. You obeyed Mommy!"

Day 215

Hold your baby in your arms and sing, "Ring Around the Rosey." When you sing, "We all fall down," bend forward and dip her so she feels the movement of the song.

> *Ring around the rosey*
> *Pocket full of posies*
> *Ashes, ashes*
> *We all fall down*

Day 216

When your baby is sitting up, set a toy slightly out of his reach so he has to walk his hands out to retrieve it. This will build his upper body strength and will help prepare him for crawling.

Day 217

Let your baby see what the world looks like from up high. Give her a ride on your shoulders, holding her securely. Watch out for low doorways! Let her look at herself sitting on your shoulders in the mirror. This is the first time she is "taller" than you are!

Reflections on the Week

Finally, brothers, whatever is true, whatever is noble, whatever is right, whatever is pure, whatever is lovely, whatever is admirable—if anything is excellent or praiseworthy—think about such things.

PHILIPPIANS 4:8

A kindhearted woman gains respect.

PROVERBS 11:16

Think Positively

There are bright moments in every day. Train your mind to focus on them. Cultivate a positive spirit in yourself. Enjoy the life God has given you. Look for things, even little ones, to thank God for. Focus on what you can do, not on what you can't. Look for the good in others; believe the best about them. Build others up, encourage them, be happy for their good fortune, and express your appreciation. Say positive things about others in conversation.

Be flexible as you handle the interruptions and mini-crises in your life. Find the humor in difficult situations. Don't take life too seriously. God will never give you more than you can handle. Don't let a toy-strewn, baby-apparatus-filled home turn you into a nagging, complaining mom. Decide on a daily basis not to complain. Mothers set the emotional thermostat for their home. How you choose to respond will determine not only your emotional well-being but also that of those around you.

Dear Lord, You are so good! Help me bring Your love and goodness into the life of others. Let all that I say, do, and think be glorifying to You. Help me always look on the bright side of things and see the good in others. Help me break my bad habits and become more and more like You. Change me so I can be Your instrument in the lives of others. Amen.

Week 32

Day 218

Now that your baby is older and stronger, you can change the motions to your "ticktock" game. Hold your baby to your chest and swing from side to side saying, "Ticktock, ticktock." Then as you say, "Cuckoo, cuckoo," lower his head and chest away from you so he is hanging almost upside down. Most babies this age love the feeling of being upside down. Make sure you support his head, neck, and back as you do this. Raise him back up and he will probably want to do it again.

Day 219

Fill your time together with happy sounds and music. Sing or hum as you go about your day. Make up silly little songs as you play with and care for your baby. Have peaceful music playing softly in your home.

Day 220

Sit on the floor and place your baby on your bent knees. Say,

1-2-3	*(bounce your baby on your knees)*
_____'s on my knee	*(bounce your baby on your knees)*
Rooster crows	*(pause)*
Cock - a - doodle - doo	*(cock-a-doodle-doo enthusiastically)*
And away she goes	*(quickly lower your knees to the floor)*

Day 221

Sit across from your baby on the floor. Roll a ball to him or toss a pair of socks (that are folded up in a ball) into his lap. When the ball lands in his lap, he will automatically touch it. Say, "Good catch!" Reach over and gently help him toss it back to you. Say, "Good throw!" Continue playing as long as he enjoys it. Your enthusiasm will make all the difference.

Day 222

Lift your baby up on her hands and knees to give her a sense of the position she will be in when she crawls. It will also help strengthen her muscles and balance.

Day 223

Teach your baby how to drink from a straw. This will come in handy if you are in a situation where he needs a little drink but you don't have a bottle or time to nurse. Put a straw in a small amount of liquid. Hold your finger on the top of the straw to trap the liquid. Let your baby suck on the straw as you release your finger.

Day 224

Sit on the floor with your legs bent and separated. Sit your baby between your legs facing you. Hold her hands. Lean forward and backward in a rowing motion while you sing "Row, Row, Row Your Boat." You can even get a mini-abdominal workout by leaning far enough back to do a reverse crunch.

Reflections on the Week

Pour out your heart like water in the presence of the LORD. Lift up your hands to him for the lives of your children.

LAMENTATIONS 2:19

As for me, far be it from me that I should sin against the LORD by failing to pray for you.

1 SAMUEL 12:23

Praying for Your Children

You are not alone in this awesome responsibility of raising children. You are in partnership with God and He is the expert. How do you have access to this expert? Through prayer. When you pray, God's power is released into your life. Prayer makes an eternal difference in the life of your children—never underestimate its power. You may see God answer your prayers by receiving wisdom, a changed attitude, or renewed hope. Rest assured that God always answers prayer in a way that is ultimately best for you.

You are called to pray for your children, to be an intercessor for them. It is a powerful resource God has given you. Your prayers will make an eternal difference in their lives. When you are anxious or distressed about your children, go to God in prayer. Pray for their character development, their safety, their faith, their future, and any other details of their lives. God loves your children even more than you do, and no prayer ever goes unanswered.

During this stage of your life, you may feel you don't have much time to pray, but prayer is something that is easily integrated into your daily life. God is always present, always available, always looking forward to hearing from you. Pray as you take your child on a walk, as you nurse or feed your baby, and as you fold the laundry. Whenever people or situations come to mind, lift them up to God in prayer. Prayer can be seamlessly woven into your day.

*D*ear *Heavenly Father, thank You that You are always available to hear and answer my prayers. I praise You that You are in complete control of my life and the life of my baby. Your power is sufficient. Thank You that You are here to help me with my parenting. Help me to be the mother You want me to be. Help me to faithfully pray for and with my child as we place our trust in You. Amen.*

Week 33

Day 225

Put on a hand puppet, and let it talk to your baby. Use different voices. Be silly, laugh, and have fun with it. Let your baby touch the puppet as it talks.

Day 226

You have probably done this many times already, but kiss your baby's precious little feet. In a couple of months, after he starts walking, his feet will never be quite so soft again. Not only will you enjoy those soft, sweet little feet, but he will enjoy it as well as he starts to notice his feet more.

Day 227

Sit on the floor. Firmly hold your baby around her chest, facing you. Say, "Let's fly through the sky." As you count to three, slowly roll backward onto your back. Gently lift your baby above you and say, "Whee, you're flying."

Day 228

In as many ways as possible, tell your baby you love her. Remember to add, "And God loves you too!"

Day 229

Cheerios are a great snack and diversion when you are out somewhere. Put some in a resealable plastic bag and keep them in your diaper bag to always have on hand.

Day 230

Place a saucepan in front of your baby. Put a small ball (big enough so it cannot fit in his mouth, but small enough for him to grasp) in the pan while he watches. Put the lid on and say, "Where's the ball?" Let him pull off the lid to discover the ball. Say, "There's the ball! It was inside the pan." Your baby will enjoy doing this while learning the concept of "inside."

Day 231

Play a xylophone for your baby. Sing the notes (do, re, mi...) as you play the notes. Try singing the song, "Do-Re-Mi" from *The Sound of Music*. Play the musical note when you sing the note's name.

Reflections on the Week

Commit everything you do to the Lord.
Trust him to help you to do it and he will.

PSALM 37:5 TLB

*Teach us to number our days aright, that
we may gain a heart of wisdom.*

PSALM 90:12

Managing Your Time

Deciding how to manage your time can be a difficult task. Being a mother is an around-the-clock job. There is no clear distinction of when you are on and when you are off duty. Having some kind of a schedule for the day will help you be in better control of your time. It will make your life easier by bringing order to your day. Life with a baby, however, is unpredictable; they have a way of not sticking to the day's agenda. So, even though it's helpful to have some kind of schedule, you must also learn to be flexible.

When planning your day, divide your projects into smaller tasks so they are more easily achievable. You will quickly gain a sense of accomplishment as you complete at least part of a project. There is something very satisfying about being able to cross a task off your to-do list. To get an even greater sense of accomplishment, write down not only the chores that need to be done, but also the important aspects of parenting. Be sure to budget in both time to work and time to play. Include activities like reading a book, playing in the tub, building a block tower, and going to the park on your to-do list. By doing this, you will be sure the truly important things get done, because any time spent playing with your baby is time well spent.

When evaluating how to allocate your time, try to distinguish between the urgent and the important. We all run around trying to busily complete what we perceive as urgent while what is truly important doesn't get our attention. Pray that God would give you wisdom in knowing which is which.

Dear Lord, help me learn to budget my time better. Show me what You consider important, what Your priorities for my life are. Help me balance the time I spend taking care of the house, caring for and playing with my baby, nurturing my relationship with my husband, and finding time for myself. I feel pulled in so many directions. Thank You, Lord, for walking with me through all this. Please give me wisdom in all I do. Amen.

Week 34

Day 232

As you go about your day, tell your baby what you are going to do before you do it. Over time, she will begin to connect the phrase with the action. For example, "Mommy has to put you down," or "Let's change your diaper," or "Up you go."

Day 233

Sit your baby in an empty box or laundry basket. Push the box around on the floor to give him a choo-choo train ride.

Day 234

Make bath time fun by letting her use some of your kitchen utensils. A turkey baster, funnel, slotted spoon, plastic measuring cup, and strainer all make wonderful playthings for the bathtub.

Day 235

Let your baby make a joyful noise unto the Lord. Give him an aluminum pie pan and spoon. Show him how to hit the spoon on the pie pan. Turn some music on and let him bang to the beat.

Day 236

Your baby will love learning the names of his body parts. Let him know that God has made every part of him by singing this song.

God made   *(touch fingers)*
_____*'s fingers*

God made   *(touch toes)*
_____*'s toes*

God made   *(touch belly button)*
_____*'s belly*
button

Round and round it   *(draw circles on tummy)*
goes

Day 237

Let your baby know how much you love her. Say, "How much does Mommy love _____?" Pause and then say, "Soooo much!" (Stretch your arms out wide). Soon she will be able to answer in the same way.

Day 238

Put a baseball hat on your head and let your baby take it off and put it back on you. She will love this game. Let her try putting it on and taking it off herself. She will probably find this more difficult.

Reflections on the Week

Consider it pure joy, my brothers, whenever you face trials of many kinds, because you know that the testing of your faith develops perseverance.

JAMES 1:2-3

We know that in all things God works for the good of those who love him, who have been called according to his purpose.

ROMANS 8:28

Learning from Our Mistakes

Are you enjoying the adventure of motherhood? Perhaps instead you are worrying so much about doing everything right that you can't just relax and enjoy your role as a mother. It is good to want to be an effective, godly mother, but don't let overzealousness rob you of the joy of parenting. God doesn't expect you to be a perfect mom. He gave you your child knowing you were inexperienced. He designed children to be able to withstand a loving parent's mistakes and shortcomings. Children are resilient and forgiving. We all make mistakes at one time or another, falling short of perfection. Learning from mistakes and failures is how we become experienced parents.

When we learn from our mistakes, instead of feeling like a failure, our children will learn that mistakes are a part of life. When we make one, it's disappointing, but not a catastrophe. When our children see that although we try, we are not perfect, they will be less likely to become frustrated perfectionists themselves. They learn that when they make a mistake, they can learn from it and move on.

Be realistic in your expectations for yourself. In public other women may look like perfect moms who have it all together, but we all have our frustrations and weaknesses. Remember we, like our children, are works in progress. God isn't finished with us yet!

Dear Lord, thank You for loving me despite my weaknesses. Thank You for this beautiful baby who also seems to just keep loving me despite my imperfections. I try so hard to be a good mom. Some days I succeed, but other days I fail miserably. Lord, when I do fail, help me learn from my mistakes. Help me to be strong in the challenges of parenting and grow through them. Amen.

Week 35

Day 239

You set the tone and atmosphere of your home with your attitude and demeanor. Model polite behavior by always saying "please" and "thank you." Try to be pleasant and calm when you interact with your baby, even when he is not. Over time you will notice him mimicking you in many ways—both your good traits and your bad! Think about the example you are setting for him.

Day 240

Clap your baby's hands together as you sing this song to the tune of "Row, Row, Row Your Boat."

Clap, clap, clap your hands
Make a pretty sound
Clap, clap, clap your hands
Now let's lay them down

Day 241

Gather any stuffed or toy animals you have. Hold up each animal, say its name, and then make its sound. You can also sing, "Old MacDonald Had a Farm" and hold up the animal as you sing about it.

Day 242

Give your baby an "Eskimo kiss" by rubbing noses together. Try a butterfly kiss by placing your eyelashes on her cheek and then blink quickly. Your fluttering lashes will gently tickle her cheek and feel like a butterfly wing.

Your Baby Is Eight Months Old!

Day 243

Place a bird feeder outside your window. When birds come to feed, pick up your baby and show him the birds. Talk about how God made many different kinds of beautiful birds.

Day 244

Help your baby learn to let go of a toy. Say, "Please give the toy to Mommy." Place your opened hand under his hand, touching the toy. This will help him relax his grip and uncurl his fingers so he is able to let go.

Day 245

Your baby can understand words long before she can say them. Give the names for things as you go about your day. When you read books, name the objects in the pictures. When possible, point out the real object in your room that you see in the book.

Reflections on the Week

Cheerfully share your home with those who need a meal or a place to stay for the night.

1 PETER 4:9 TLB

Share with God's people who are in need. Practice hospitality.

ROMANS 12:13

Practicing Hospitality

We want our homes to be a place where people feel welcome. As we make new friends and nurture old friendships, we can practice the virtue of hospitality. There is a difference between entertaining and hospitality. Entertaining is often about trying to impress our guests by showing off our homes and culinary skills. It usually requires much work and is not easy to do with a baby in tow.

Hospitality, on the other hand, focuses on opening our homes to others, making them feel comfortable and welcome. We want everyone who comes to our homes to feel like a special guest. Because we are not worried about impressing them, we can relax and enjoy their friendship. Hospitality allows us to build relationships. It also teaches our children how to socialize and get along with others.

Now I confess, the minute I know that someone is coming over, my tendency is to go into cleaning overdrive. I have to remind myself that people are not expecting my house to look like a model home. Six people live here, and there are going to be signs of it. We need to be more interested in our guests than in the cleanliness of our homes. To save time, just clean up the rooms where your guests will be and forget about the rest.

It also helps to keep your food as simple as possible. The important element in hospitality is what goes on *around* the table, rather than what's on it or how it is set. Have a family over for ice cream sundaes after dinner or for bagels and cream cheese after church. Make a salad and have a pizza delivered. Buy a loaf of French bread and heat up a pot of homemade soup or chili that you have frozen. Laugh, tell stories, and share a part of your life as you enjoy each other's friendship.

Dear Lord, I want to have friends over more often, but the mere thought of it is overwhelming. Help me not to worry about making sure everything is perfect. Help me instead to focus on loving others, enjoying their fellowship, and making them feel welcome. Amen.

Week 36

Day 246

Turn on some music. Kneel in front of your baby. Hold him under his arms so he is standing. Move your body to the music and help him dance with you. When he tires of this, pick him up and dance around the room with him.

Day 247

Sing to the tune of "He's Got the Whole World in His Hands."

> *Mommy loves _____, yes I do*
> *Oh, Mommy loves _____, yes I do*
> *Oh, Mommy loves _____, yes I do*
> *Oh, Mommy loves _____*
> _____ (first and last names or first and middle names so the correct number of syllables fit into the song)

Day 248

It's not too early to begin teaching your baby to pick up after himself. Say, "It's time to clean up now," and begin picking up. Help him to hold onto a toy and place it where it belongs. When you are finished, say, "Thank you for helping me clean up!" This instills a sense of orderliness and responsibility. At the beginning you will be doing most of the work as you model what "clean up" means, but in the long run it will pay off as he learns to do it on his own.

Day 249

When you are dressing your baby say, "I love your nose," and give her nose a kiss. Then, "I love your tummy, cheeks, toes, etc." kissing each body part as you say it.

Day 250

Next time you or your husband calls home, let your baby "talk" on the telephone too. Listening to a familiar voice over the phone, when he can't see the person, is quite a novelty for him.

Day 251

Lay your baby in the middle of a large blanket on the floor. Gently pull the edges of the blanket and give her a magic carpet ride. This is a lot of fun and helps develop her balance.

Day 252

Say "beep, beep, beep" slowly as you move your face closer to your baby's face. When you get close enough, rub noses and say, "beep, beep, beep" quickly. Your baby will love the anticipation of what's to come.

Reflections for the Week

He commanded our forefathers to teach their children, so the next generation would know them, even the children yet to be born, and they in turn would tell their children. Then they would put their trust in God and would not forget his deeds but would keep his commands.

PSALM 78:5-7

A wise teacher makes learning a joy.

PROVERBS 15:2 TLB

Teach Your Children

You are your baby's first teacher. As a mother, this will be your primary role over the next twenty plus years. You are getting off to a great start nurturing your baby's development by doing the activities in this book. Babies learn through repetition, so repeat the games, and songs over and over with him. Have fun while you are doing it because your baby will learn best in the context of a loving relationship. The goal is not to produce a child prodigy, but to gently nuture his natural development.

You also have the privilege of teaching your baby about love, faith, and forgiveness. And language, music, and art. And manners, respect, and responsibility. The list goes on and on. Sometimes without even noticing it, you are teaching him many, many lessons throughout the day.

When your little one is young, you will spend much time with him. Make these moments count because the time will come when he will enter school and you will have fewer hours to spend together. At the end of his childhood, you will need to release him to be on his own. When that day comes, you want to meet it with no regrets over lessons not learned or time not well spent.

Dear God, it seems every day my baby is learning something new. It is amazing how much he has already changed in these few short months. Help me to be a good teacher. Help me to make good use of those teachable moments when I can begin to teach him about You. Help me to be patient, creative, and fun as I teach and train my child. Amen.

Week 37

Day 253

Hand your baby two small blocks, one for each hand. Now hand her a third block. She will have to drop one block in order to take the third block from you. This will help her practice letting go of an object.

Day 254

Sit your baby on your knees, facing you. Hold her torso. Bounce her as you say, "1, 2, 3." Then separate your knees and let her drop down a couple of inches between your legs and say, "Whoops a daisy."

Day 255

When your baby puts something in his mouth that he shouldn't, say, "Yuck!" and take it out. He will learn that when you say "yuck," he shouldn't be putting the object in his mouth. This helps in two ways. "Yuck" is an easy word to learn, so if you are not right next to him to pull the object out, he will know that he needs to spit out whatever he has in his mouth. It also gives you an alternative word for "no," so you don't have to use it so much.

Remember when he obeys, to give him lots of praise and say, "Good job! You obeyed Mommy."

Day 256

Put a small object in the palm of your hand. Slowly curl your fingers over it while your baby watches. Ask your baby where it went. Let her open up your fingers to find the object. She is learning that even though she cannot see something, it is still there—object permanence.

Day 257

Sit on the floor with your baby. Throw a light scarf into the air and let it float down. The next time, catch it as it comes down. You can hold your baby's hand out to help him catch it also.

Day 258

Start your baby's day off with a happy song. Sing:

Rise and shine and give God the glory, glory
Rise and shine and give God the glory, glory
Rise and shine and give God the glory, glory
Children of the Lord!

Day 259

Take your baby to the playground. Let him run his fingers through the sand and bury his toes in it. Bring plastic cups for him to practice filling and pouring the sand.

Reflections on the Week

Come to me, all you who are weary and burdened, and I will give you rest. Take my yoke upon you and learn from me, for I am gentle and humble in heart, and you will find rest for your souls.

MATTHEW 11:28-29

My grace is sufficient for you, for my power is made perfect in weakness.

2 CORINTHIANS 12:9

Overwhelmed and Exhausted

Do you feel overwhelmed, unappreciated, and thoroughly exhausted? Raising children and maintaining a household can be physically tiring, emotionally exhausting, and incredibly time consuming. It may seem as though your work is never complete, and when you do manage to complete a task, it never stays finished for long. Parenting is hard work, but don't let the difficulties overshadow the incredible blessings that come with it. No other job is as meaningful or as important as raising and training your children. Sometimes it's helpful to stop and realize the eternal significance of what you are doing.

You are not alone in your weariness; God is right there with you. Trust in His strength. God didn't give you this incredibly important and challenging job and expect you to do it on your own. He wants you to go to Him for rest and strength and wisdom. You cannot be the mother He wants you to be depending solely on your own strength. He'll work through your weaknesses and insecurities by His supernatural power. Lean on God, depend on Him. He can accomplish great things through you!

Dear God, my baby often needs me around the clock. Weariness seems to be my constant companion. I keep waiting for things to "get back to normal," but I am beginning to realize this is normal now. Help me to remember the eternal value of what I am doing. Please give me an extra dose of energy and patience today to care for my sweet child. Amen.

Week 38

Day 260

It may seem too early to start thinking about it now, but part of your job as a parent is to train your child in right behavior. It is easier to train your child correctly the first time than to have to correct her later after you have allowed a bad behavior to become acceptable. You can begin by teaching her to take care of her toys. Don't let her throw her toys across the room. Say, "No, we need to take care of our toys." Self-control is an important character trait to work on from the beginning.

Day 261

Purchase a children's Bible storybook intended for babies or toddlers. Read a Bible story every night at bedtime. It is never too early to begin storing God's Word in your baby's heart.

Day 262

Your baby is becoming more dexterous with his hands and will enjoy squishing and squeezing these tactile bags. Fill a plastic bag with Jell-O and seal it. Let him experiment with poking, squeezing, and pounding the

Jell-O inside the bag. Be careful that he doesn't put the bag in his mouth. Try using different ingredients, such as pudding, crushed ice cubes, or a water and cornstarch mixture.

Day 263

When your pediatrician gives you a prescription, ask the nurse if she or someone else in the office can call it in to the pharmacy. You won't have to wait as long with your sick baby for the pharmacy to fill your prescription. Choose one pharmacy that you like and always use it so you won't have to give your insurance information each time you go.

Day 264

Begin teaching sharing early. If your baby hands you one of his toys, say, "Oh, thank you for sharing with me." When you are playing with him ask, "Can Mommy have a turn now? Thank you. What a good sharer you are!" Be sure to give the toy back quickly to him at first. He will begin to learn that his toys will not be gone forever if someone else has them.

Day 265

Get a good first aid book for childhood emergencies and review it often. Being prepared will help you not to panic because you will know what to do and where to quickly turn for specific information. You should be certified in infant and child CPR. Check with your pediatrician or hospital for classes. Another important thing to do is to post the dosage charts for ibuprofen (Motrin) and acetaminophen (Tylenol) (available from your pediatrician) inside your medicine cabinet door so you can be sure to administer the right amount of medicine as your baby's weight changes.

Day 266

In all your efforts to be a wonderful mother, don't forget you are a wife too. Never stop loving your husband. It is the best gift you can give your baby.

Reflections on the Week

Love the LORD your God with all your heart and with all your soul and with all your strength. These commandments that I give you today are to be upon your hearts. Impress them on your children. Talk about them when you sit at home and when you walk along the road, when you lie down and when you get up.

DEUTERONOMY 6:5-7

Fathers, do not exasperate your children; instead, bring them up in the training and instruction of the Lord.

EPHESIANS 6:4

Character Development

You have spent the first months of motherhood loving your baby, caring for her, and enjoying every precious moment with her. You have built a wonderful foundation of love, trust, and nurturing. As your baby grows older, you will assume a new responsibility—her moral training. Unfortunately, godly character traits don't naturally appear in children. They must be developed, directed, and shaped over many years. This is one of the most important jobs you will have as a mother. You need to build her character and shape her personality on a day-to-day basis. It is a process that doesn't take just one time, but comes from hundreds of ten-second lessons taught throughout the day. Each time a little bit more settles in. The results aren't immediate, but if you persevere, and with God's help, you will see results.

As you diligently teach God's ways to your children, you are establishing guidelines and principles that will help them throughout their lives. Their future success in school, work, and life will be determined by the quality of their character. This is not at all about trying to manip- ulate their personalities to be how you want them to be. Instead, you are working with the strengths and weaknesses of their God-given temperament, helping them grow into the people God intends them to be.

*D*ear Lord, wow, what a responsibility You have given my husband and me to mold our child's character to be pleasing to You. I am not sure how to do it or when to begin, but I do know that I want to raise children who "turn out right." I want to raise children who know You, love You, and follow Your ways. Please, Lord, help me to know how to do this. Instruct me in Your Word, introduce me to experienced mothers who can model it for me, and help me find books that give godly wisdom in this area. Thank You that I am not in this alone; I've got You, God. Amen.

Week 39

Day 267

Sit with your baby and hold her hands. Say, "How big is _____?" Then say, "Soooo big" as you raise her arms high. Do it yourself and then let her copy you.

Day 268

Tie a ribbon around your baby's favorite toy (only leave six inches for her to pull). Show her how to pull the ribbon to move the toy closer. When she is able to do this well, hide the toy around a corner or under a blanket with only the ribbon showing. Let her pull the ribbon to find the toy.

Day 269

Help develop your baby's imagination by introducing him to pretend play. Put out some pots, pans, spoons, and lids. Show him how to pretend to cook. If he enjoys this, it can be a great distraction for him when you are trying to make dinner.

Day 270

Talk, talk, talk to your baby. This will help his language development. Do it in a fun, natural way. Use short but complete sentences. Repeat back the sounds he makes to you. Be enthusiastic and animated. Talk about things as you are doing them. Ask him questions and wait long enough for him to "answer." Your baby already understands much more of what you say than you probably realize! Help him build his vocabulary by naming toys and objects as you see or play with them. Try to use the same word each time you refer to the same object.

Day 271

Your baby loves to imitate you. Play follow the leader and let your baby do these activities after you—shake your head, cluck your tongue, clap your hands, smack your lips, blow raspberries, wave bye-bye, and blow a kiss.

Day 272

Next time you finish a cereal box, save it. Open both ends. Show your baby how to push a car through the box to make it come out the other side. Show her how the car can go in, be hidden for a moment, and then reappear!

Day 273

As your baby becomes more mobile, you will need to teach him what the word "no" means. Put away anything unsafe or valuable, but it is okay to leave some things out around your house that he is not allowed to handle. It is important for him to learn that there are some things that are not for him to touch. Learning to obey when you say, "No, don't touch" will help keep your baby safe and begin to teach him self-control and respect for other people's property.

Your Baby Is Nine Months Old!

Reflections of the Week

The wise woman builds her house, but with her own hands the foolish one tears hers down.

PROVERBS 14:1

*Pleasant words are a honeycomb, sweet
to the soul and healing to the bones.*

PROVERBS 16:24

Creating the Atmosphere

As a mother you can bring warmth and acceptance into your home by creating a loving atmosphere. A home that is filled with love, joy, laughter, encouragement, and forgiveness doesn't just happen automatically. You must consciously work on it, but the reward is that your children will have the blessing of growing up in a happy, loving home. Set the mood and maintain the atmosphere by encouraging each other, focusing on the good, and making each person feel loved and special.

Your disposition has a great impact on the atmosphere in your home. Your children's attitude is often determined by your own. Watch out for the tone of your voice. Is it sarcastic, cynical, or condescending? Do you speak to family members with the same tone you would use with a visiting friend? One of the easiest ways to enhance the atmosphere of your home is to smile often. A smile says, "I love you, I like being with you, you are important to me!" A warm smile makes anyone feel better.

How you manage your home also helps set the atmosphere. Play music that is fun, peaceful, or uplifting. Display photos of happy times spent together. Maintain some semblance of order in your home. Make ordinary days seem extra special. Try lighting candles at dinnertime or placing a vase of fresh flowers in your family room. Be creative in enhancing the atmosphere of your home, making it warm and inviting.

Dear Lord, there is so much more to motherhood than I ever thought! Help me to create a warm and loving atmosphere in my home. Let my family be characterized by peace, love, and acceptance. I know it has to start with me, Lord. Please help me set the tone by how I respond to my husband and children. Let my words build others up, not tear them down. Work through me, God, so I can bring beauty and love into our home. Amen.

The Fourth
Three Months

A Bundle of Energy

When I approach a child,
he inspires in me two sentiments:
tenderness for what he is, and
respect for what he may become.

LOUIS PASTEUR

Week 40

Day 274

Sit in front of a mirror with your baby sitting between your legs. Sing this song to the tune of "Here We Go Round the Mulberry Bush."

This is the way we   (touch your baby's nose)
touch our nose

Touch our nose, touch   (touch your baby's nose)
our nose

This is the way we   (touch your baby's nose)
touch our nose

Early in the morning   (clap to the beat)

Sing a few more verses using different body parts each time.

Day 275

Practice showing your baby how to sit back down after she learns how to pull herself up to a standing position. It will be easier for her to learn how to stand up than to sit down. She may practice pulling herself up in her crib at naptime and will then be stuck because she can't get back down. Now that she has mastered this skill, set her crib to the lowest position. Make sure there are no pillows or large toys for her to stand on so she can't fall out.

Day 276

Your baby is nine months old already! Pull out your audiotape and record your baby's sounds, laughter, and babbling. Sometimes her jabbering will sound like a real conversation!

It's time for your baby's
nine-month checkup

Day 277

Now that your baby is probably moving about, there will be plenty of minor bumps and bruises. Your reaction to these will affect his response. Stay calm and matter-of-fact, saying, "Whoops you fell down! You're okay, let's get up again." Kiss his "owie" to make it all better again. If you overreact, he probably will too. Of course, when he does have a hard fall, you will want to hold him in your arms and gently comfort him.

Day 278

Your baby has watched you answer the telephone many times. Now let her have the opportunity to use a play telephone. Make a ringing sound. Pretend to answer and tell her that the call is for her. Give her the phone and help her hold the receiver to her ear to say "Hello."

Day 279

A colorful beach ball is an inexpensive toy for your baby with many entertaining uses. You can roll it back and forth to each other. He can hit it with his hand and crawl after it. You can lay his body over it and roll the ball gently back and forth for a fun ride.

Day 280

Lay a few sofa cushions on the floor. Let your baby be a mountain climber, crawling up and over them. She will enjoy the challenge of learning to balance her body in new ways as she climbs, crawls, and slides over them.

Reflections on the Week

There is a time for everything, and a season for every activity under heaven.

ECCLESIASTES 3:1

Those who have served well gain an excellent standing and great assurance in their faith in Christ Jesus.

1 TIMOTHY 3:13

Determining Your Priorities

Before you had children, you were probably able to accomplish many things. Now it may seem as though you are busy all day but not accomplishing much of anything. You don't have time to get caught up on daily work or pursue outside interests. Take heart, this season of life won't last forever. For now though, you may need to scale back on some of your outside commitments—volunteer work, ministry opportunities, special projects, and so on. It's helpful to pace yourself by not saying yes to every opportunity that comes along. Determine what your priorities are and then make decisions accordingly.

You simply can't be an effective mother if you are trying to do too many other things. Parenting is a full-time job. When you become overcommitted, your family members are usually the ones who suffer the most. There will be many years for you to complete your list of projects and do volunteer work. Right now your children are your work, your main ministry. There is no greater way for you to serve God than to nurture your children with love and patience. Say no to many *good* things so you have time and energy left for the *best* thing—your children. These days with your baby will pass by quickly; make each one count!

*D*ear *Lord, there are so many things I would like to do, but I never seem to find the time. Help me to have a servant's heart that lovingly gives up or delays some of my desires so I can invest myself in the life of my baby. Please give me wisdom in knowing when to say yes and when to say no to outside commitments, even ones that seem so worthwhile. Amen.*

Week 41

Day 281

Give your baby two blocks, one for each hand. Pick up two of your own and show him how to bang them together. Encourage him to copy you. Bang them slowly then quickly, quietly then loudly, and to the beat of music.

Day 282

When you have decided that something is off limits for your baby to touch, be consistent. Make sure you enforce your "no" in a firm (this isn't the same as mean, angry, or loud) voice each time he touches it. Don't pretend to not notice him touching it because you are too tired or too busy to stop him. That will send a mixed message that "sometimes Mommy lets me touch it and other times not." If he doesn't obey, move him away. Don't just keep repeating yourself. It takes more effort now, but will pay off in the long run when he knows what things are off limits to him and that your "no" means no. Remember this is a process. He is still very young and training takes time, love, and patience.

Day 283

Play beauty parlor with your baby. Using her baby brush, show her how you brush your hair, then brush her hair. Hand her the brush and let her brush your hair and then her own hair.

Day 284

Give your baby a pot and two lids—one that fits and one that doesn't. See if she can discover which lid fits the pot. Bring out the other matching pot. Let her practice putting the lids on and off.

Day 285

Give your baby two plastic measuring cups. Show her how to place one inside the other. Give her the smallest cup and let her try. When she can accomplish this, give her a third cup. Use the words "large" and "small" as you do this with her.

Day 286

Let him touch cold things throughout the day. As he touches them, say "cold" in a shaky voice as if you were cold. Try touching the inside of the refrigerator, a cold windowpane, cold water, or cold food at the grocery store.

Day 287

Help your baby develop a sense of rhythm. Sing a song and clap your hands or tap your fingers to the rhythm on the table.

Reflections on the Week

I have learned to be content whatever the circumstances. I know what it is to be in need, and I know what it is to have plenty. I have learned the secret of being content in any and every situation, whether well fed or hungry, whether living in plenty or in want.

PHILIPPIANS 4:11-12

Keep your lives free from the love of money and be content with what you have, because God has said, "Never will I leave you; never will I forsake you."

HEBREWS 13:5

Living in Contentment

Do you ever find yourself comparing your life with others? Longing for things you cannot have? Wishing your life was somehow different? We all struggle with contentment at one time or another. Often the things we think will make us happy are just temporary fixes. There is always one more thing we need to get or make happen before we can be truly happy.

To be content, we need to have God's perspective and be thankful for what He has already given us. We often take for granted the many blessings that surround us. We need to focus on the positive, not the negative; on what we have, not on what we don't have.

Take a moment and list all the positive things about your financial situation, your husband, your baby's temperament, your appearance, your living arrangements, or whatever it is that causes you to be discontent. Then focus on God's blessings in your life. Get in the habit of telling God daily what you are thankful for, because contentment usually comes more from a change in our attitude than from a change in our circumstances.

Dear God, I praise You and thank You for all You have given me. You are always so faithful! Forgive me, Lord, for the times when I am discontent. It can be so easy to focus on the negative instead of the positive. Teach me to be content in every circumstance by focusing on Your blessings in my life. I know that You can work all things together for my good. Help me take my eyes off myself and place them instead on You. Amen.

Week 42

Day 288

Turn on a musical toy for your baby and hide it in the room. Say, "Where's the music? Let's go find it." Look several places saying, "Is it here? No, it's not here. Let's listen again." On the second or third try, find it together. After some practice, let your baby try to find it on her own.

Day 289

Let your baby hear you counting to give her a beginning understanding of numbers. Count her fingers and toes. Count pushes on the swing. Count blocks as you build them, socks as you fold them, and cups of water as you pour them into the bathtub.

Day 290

When you have told your child not to touch something, give him the opportunity to obey. Say no and act confidently that he will obey. Children will often live up or down to your expectations. Move away and give him a chance to change his course of action (of course, don't do this if it involves a safety issue). Don't stand and stare him down. He may see this as a challenge and disobey just to see what will happen. Praise him when he chooses to obey.

Day 291

Bumps and bruises are an inevitable part of childhood. Be prepared by keeping a couple frozen ketchup packages (from fast food restaurants) on hand. They are the perfect size cold packs for covering bumps and bruises on small children, and they stay squishy even when frozen.

Day 292

The fact that things still exist, even when we can't see them, is a budding new concept for your baby. Let him experience it with this game. Drop a toy into a paper bag with your baby watching. Say, "Where is the toy?" Let him delight in finding it.

Day 293

Give your baby time to explore on her own. It's tempting to do everything for her so she never experiences any frustration. There are times, however, when it is good to give her opportunities to solve problems and figure out solutions on her own without your guidance. She will feel a sense of pride as she does this.

Day 294

Your baby will love crawling up steps. Give him plenty of time to practice. He will delight in his sense of accomplishment. Always be right there behind him, as he doesn't yet realize he can't just sit back down. You may even let him fall back part of the way before you catch him so he will learn what will happen in a controlled setting.

Reflections on the Week

Train a child in the way he should go, and when he is old he will not turn from it.

PROVERBS 22:6

Let us not become weary in doing good, for at the proper time we will reap a harvest if we do not give up.

GALATIANS 6:9

The Moral Training of Our Children

As you begin morally training your child in what is right and wrong behavior, you may sometimes become overzealous and easily frustrated. Occasionally, despite your efforts, you may feel as though you are taking two steps forward, then one step back. Try to remind yourself that this is a long process (as we all well know, based on the areas we still need to work on ourselves!). The training you are doing now is a worthwhile investment.

Don't give up. The seeds you are planting will begin to bear fruit in the very near future.

Begin working on proper behavior by focusing on just a few areas that need attention. It's easier to instill good habits one at a time. When you decide to work on a specific behavior issue, stay consistent in enforcing it. Give your child lots of encouragement. Look for good behavior to applaud by focusing on what he is doing right.

You can build good character while respecting their unique personalities. Sometimes what you see as a character flaw is just a positive trait that needs a little refinement. For example, help your stubborn child to become persistent and your overly sensitive child to become compassionate. All you're doing here is modifying their natural bent to a more positive attribute. In this way you will bring out the best in your child while still allowing his unique personality to flourish.

Dear Lord, please give me wisdom in knowing how to morally train my child. Help me know how to encourage her to be kind, gentle, patient, and characterized by self-control. Help me to develop these same virtues in my own life so I can lead by example. Please help me keep a proper perspective. Help me realize that she is just a young child, so that I don't set my expectations too high. Amen.

Week 43

Day 295

When you come across special things in your home that belong to others, point it out to your child. Say, "This is Daddy's wallet," or "sister's doll." Begin teaching her the concept of ownership. Your child will slowly begin to learn that everything is not hers to play with.

Day 296

Your body is an exciting crawling apparatus for your baby. Your legs and torso make great hills for him to climb over or sit on. When you laugh, it will make your stomach rise and fall to your baby's delight.

Day 297

Your baby will make a mess as he learns to eat finger foods. It takes awhile to develop the eye-hand coordination to get the food directly into his mouth. However, don't allow your baby to purposely drop or throw his food on the ground just to see what happens or because he doesn't want anymore. He has plenty of opportunities throughout the day to discover the joys of dropping things to see what happens. Food doesn't have to be one of those things.

> Don't give your baby these finger foods as they can cause choking: popcorn, raw carrots, hot dogs, nuts, apples, whole grapes.

Day 298

It's never too early to begin teaching good manners. Teach your baby some social graces such as waving bye-bye, saying "hi" with a smile, and blowing a kiss. Encourage her to use these when she is with other people.

Day 299

Here is a prayer for those especially difficult days:

Dear Lord,

Give me patience when tiny hands
Tug at me with their small demands.

Give me gentle, smiling eyes.
Keep my lips from sharp replies.

Let not fatigue, confusion, or noise
Obscure my vision of life's fleeting joys

So years later, when my house is still—
No bitter memories its rooms may fill.

AUTHOR UNKNOWN

Day 300

Be careful not to focus solely on your baby's physical and intellectual developments without also focusing on his character development. Raising him to be morally good will take much time, work, and patience. There are times when he will not be able to have his way, and that will make him angry. If you always give in to avoid any conflict, it is just postponing the inevitable. Self-control is difficult to learn, but it only comes with practice. Take the time to instill good habits now.

Day 301

Play your first game of hide-and-seek with your baby. Play in teams, with Daddy helping. Hide behind a chair in the room and say, "Here I am, _____. Come find Mommy." Let her find you by listening to your voice. Make some noise as she looks for you. Now let your husband and her hide together for you to find.

Reflections on the Week

Do not let this Book of the Law depart from your mouth; meditate on it day and night, so that you may be careful to do everything written in it.

JOSHUA 1:8

The whole Bible was given to us by inspi-
ration from God and is useful to teach us
what is true and to make us realize what
is wrong in our lives; it straightens us out
and helps us do what is right.

2 Timothy 3:16 tlb

Spending Time in God's Word

The Bible is not a book of dry history filled with outdated ideas. It is more than a collection of stories. It is truly relevant to our daily lives. The Bible is a personal letter written to each one of us from God. It guides us in how we should live, shapes our values, and offers us comfort and encouragement. We do not read the Bible only to gather information, but to have our lives transformed. When we begin to regularly read God's Word, we start to see that change. As mothers, we often realize how far away from God's ideal we are, yet God will help us grow to become more like Him. When we apply His Word to our lives, it causes us to grow and change.

The first step in reading your Bible is to find a version that will work for you. Look for a version that is written in everyday language so it is easy to understand. A study or application Bible that has footnotes will help you better understand the text and apply it to your life. Once you have a Bible, try to spend at least five or ten minutes a day reading it. Find a time that works for you—in the morning, during one of your baby's feedings, or before you go to bed at night. Sometimes it is hard to know where to start reading. You can use a devotional guide or just pick a book of the Bible, like Proverbs or James. They both have practical advice for daily living.

Your faith will grow as you spend time in the Bible. As you read, ask yourself, "How can this apply to my life today? What is God trying to teach me?" Be willing to change when God reveals to you an area of your life that needs some work. The more time you spend in God's Word, the more your thoughts will become like His thoughts, your responses like His responses, and your love like His love. Reading God's Word will transform your life and help you to become the mother He wants you to be.

Dear Lord, thank You for speaking to me through the Bible. Please help me find the time to read Your Word. Direct me to just the right passage that can offer me hope, encouragement, wisdom, and maybe even conviction if I need it. I want to grow closer to You and know You better. I want to be a reflection of You to my children. Amen.

Week 44

Day 302

Your baby is able to sit still and take a real interest in books now. Read to him often. Books that have just one or two words per page are good for vocabulary building. He will also enjoy books that have a short rhyming text.

Day 303

Your baby has an insatiable curiosity. Play a fun game with her by wrapping a small toy in three or four layers of paper (just fold the paper, don't tape it). Let her unwrap it and see what treasure is inside.

Your Baby Is Ten Months Old!

Day 304

Help teach your baby to be loving and gentle. Give him a baby doll or teddy bear. Show him how to cradle the doll in his arms and rock it. Sing a lullaby. Use the word "gentle" as you demonstrate it for him. Hug his doll and say, "Mommy is hugging the baby. Can you hug the baby?" Praise him for his gentleness.

Day 305

Tie a beach ball to a string and attach it to the top of the doorway. Adjust the length so the ball is at face level when your baby is sitting. She will enjoy hitting it and watching it swing back and forth. Always stay right with your baby to supervise her when she is using the long string. Take it down and put the string away as soon as you are finished.

Day 306

Here is a game that helps develop your baby's memory skills and shows him that something is still there even when he can't see it. Give him a toy and ask him to give it back to you. While he is watching, hide the toy under a pillow. Say, "Where's the toy?" Let him find it. At first you may need to leave part of the toy exposed. When he finds it say, "You found the toy!"

Day 307

Make a fort for you and your baby. Drape a blanket over the back of several chairs. Have fun sitting in it and crawling in and out of it. Enjoy a snack together in your tent.

Day 308

Establish a soothing bedtime routine. Help your baby learn to unwind. Even though you may be exhausted and just want some time to yourself, try to make this a special, pleasant time of day.

Reflections on the Week

In everything set them an example by doing what is good. In your teaching show integrity, seriousness and sound-ness of speech that cannot be con-demned.

TITUS 2:7

Follow God's example in everything you do just as a much loved child imitates his father.

EPHESIANS 5:1 TLB

Lead by Your Example

It has been said that children learn best from example; the trouble is they don't know a good example from a bad one! Actions speak louder than words. Your children observe everything you do and say, unconsciously absorbing it all. They are processing and storing more information than you may realize. What a responsibility you have! The example you provide for them is what will be imprinted on their character. Your baby is a great student and imitator of you—down to your unconscious mannerisms. Soon he will be repeating back your actions, words, expressions, and tones of voice. Will you like what you see and hear? He is following in your footsteps.

God's strength is there to help you model a life of love, joy, peace, patience, kindness, goodness, faithfulness, gentleness, and self-control. These are what are called the "fruit of the Spirit." They are character traits that come from walking closely with God—knowing, loving, and imitating Him. Take care to sow good seeds into your child's life because "the apple doesn't fall far from the tree"!

*D*ear God, I want to be a good example to my child. I don't want her to pick up bad habits from watching me. Please help me be characterized by the qualities I want to see blossom in my child's life. I can't do this solely in my own strength; I need to be filled with Your Holy Spirit. Transform my life so I can be a reflection of You to my children. Amen.

Week 45

Day 309

Your baby will love mimicking you as you play this game. Use four unbreakable coasters and take turns handing the coasters back and forth. Next, clap your two coasters together and let her clap hers together. Place one of your coasters on your head and ask her to put one on her head too. Share lots of praise and laughter.

Day 310

Help your baby learn to go down stairs safely. Sit him at the top of the staircase and help him move to the position of laying on his tummy, with his feet leading the way. Verbally remind him, "Feet first, on your tummy." Help him learn to back his way down. This will take some practice, as it is the opposite motion of climbing up the stairs, which comes more naturally.

Day 311

Baby food meat in a jar often doesn't taste very good on its own. Try spreading a thin layer of baby food meat on a slice of bread or a cracker to make it more appealing.

Day 312

Help your baby learn to take turns. Roll a ball back and forth saying, "It's Mommy's turn. Now it's _____'s turn. " She will enjoy playing ball with you, so "taking turns" will just come naturally with this game as she begins to understand the concept.

Day 313

Take your baby to the zoo. Don't try to see every animal on this trip. Focus instead on animals that are large, close enough to see, and very active. The primate (monkey) area is often a favorite spot. Don't forget to also visit the petting zoo.

Day 314

Simple everyday objects often make the best toys. Try using an empty paper towel or toilet paper roll as a megaphone. Talk to your baby through it or make a trumpet sound. Let her have a try.

Day 315

Take your baby outside when it is sunny and show him his shadow. Let him move and watch what his shadow does. Your baby will be intrigued by how his shadow follows him. Move around and let him watch your shadow too.

Reflections on the Week

A cheerful look brings joy to the heart.

PROVERBS 15:30

I praise you, Father, LORD of heaven and earth, because you have hidden these things from the wise and learned, and revealed them to little children

MATTHEW 11:25

Enjoy Your Child's World

Children are a gift to enjoy and nurture. Take time occasionally to retreat from the hectic world around you and leisurely enter your child's world. When those moments come (and they come often) when your child wants to play or sing a song or read a book, you sometimes need to stop whatever chore you are doing and take the time to play. Set aside your to-do list, give him your full attention, and enjoy the moment. Take a slow walk to explore spiderwebs, snail shells, shiny rocks, or a line of marching ants. Marvel at God's creation together through the eyes of your child. Be spontaneous, freely join in his silliness, and delight in his joy. Dance around the room or sing a song pretending you are up on stage. You will never have a more appreciative audience.

Make cookies and let your child clumsily pour ingredients into the bowl and stir the batter. The "successful" completion of the activity is not what is important, but instead it is the time you spend together.

Sometimes you need to slow down long enough just to sit and watch your baby play or peacefully sleep. You spend so much time interacting and caring for your baby that it can be enjoyable just to sit back and watch him from afar as he entertains himself or interacts with someone else. Treasure the moments you spend together. They are the foundation on which your relationship is being built.

Dear Lord, help me not get so caught up in caring for my baby that I neglect to just enjoy him as a person. Help me to slow down and enter into my child's unhurried world. Help me to find joy in the simple things in life and to see the world through my child's eyes. Thank You, Lord, for this child and all the important things he is teaching me. Amen.

Week 46

Day 316

Your baby understands much more than he is able to speak. This can be frustrating to him as he tries to communicate his needs to you. You can teach him several words in sign language to give him an alternative to crying or screaming to get across his message. Just learning the sign for "more," "all done," "please," and "thank you" will be a great help to him in communicating with you. Teach him just one word at a time. Sign the word whenever you say it. Help your baby to sign the word whenever he could be using it. Within a month or so, he will be using the words as he needs them.

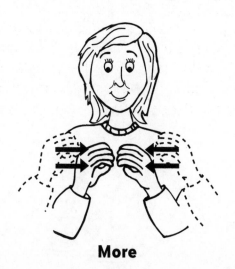

More

All done

Please

Thank you

Day 317

Spread a large towel on the kitchen floor or go outside if it is warm. Fill a shallow pan with lukewarm water. Give your baby a plastic cup, a spoon, and a washcloth. She will love to play with the water. This activity can keep her busy for a long time, but never leave her alone with even a small amount of standing water.

Day 318

Prop one end of your ironing board on a kitchen chair to make a hill for cars to go down (this may be the only use of your ironing board these days!). Collect any little cars he may have. Show him how to roll a car by saying, "One, two, three, go!" and let the car go down the ramp. Let the cars race each other. Older siblings will love to demonstrate this for him.

Day 319

Place some special, early morning toys in the far end of your baby's crib after she has gone to sleep at night. When she wakes up in the morning, she will be delighted to find them. The toys will often entertain your baby for a long time while allowing you to get some extra sleep. Rotate the toys to keep her crib playtime interesting and intriguing. Be *especially* careful to make sure none of the toys has any small parts that could cause choking. Also be sure they aren't large enough to allow her to use them as a step stool to climb out of the crib.

Day 320

Help keep messes to a minimum when your baby is eating drippy foods such as watermelon or Popsicles. Slip terry cloth ponytail holders over his wrists to absorb the juice and keep it from running down his arms. Another trick to try with Popsicles is to put a small beverage container top from a fast food restaurant or a top from a sippy cup onto the stick. The lid will catch most of the juice.

Day 321

Your child's teddy bear can help teach her what it means to obey. Tell the teddy bear, "Come to Mommy," and have Teddy scurry over to you. Praise the bear with a hug and say, "Good job! You obeyed Mommy." Think of other things you could ask him to do, such as, "Give _____ a hug," and then praise Teddy again for obeying you.

Day 322

When you go to the grocery store, talk about what you are getting, where you are going next, and things you see in the aisles. He will love seeing all the sights and hearing the new sounds.

Reflections on the Week

Discipline your son, and he will give you peace; he will bring delight to your soul.

PROVERBS 29:17

He who loves [his child] is careful to discipline him.

PROVERBS 13:24

The Need to Discipline

"My child is just a baby. It is too early to start teaching her right from wrong."

"If I discipline her, she won't love me as much."

"It is too much work, and, besides, she won't understand what we are trying to teach her. I'll wait until she is older."

All of these sentences convey understandable feelings, yet none of them is true. It is not enough just to love our children; we must also train and discipline them. Discipline sounds like such a harsh word, yet it simply means helping them learn right from wrong. It is first and foremost about teaching, not punishing. We have all seen, and perhaps even know, rude, disrespectful, and disobedient children. Children who just aren't pleasant to be around. No one wants their child to be that way; however, well-behaved children don't just turn out on their own. It is our responsibility as parents to begin laying the foundation for our children's moral and character development. When we discipline them, it is an expression of love. It will help them live lives that are honoring to God.

Discipline is one of the most difficult and draining parts of parenting, but it is worth the effort in the long run. Life with undisciplined children is frustrating and chaotic. When we discipline, we are helping our children to learn self-control, obedience, and respect. Other people will enjoy being around them. They will do better at school and on the playground. Discipline is a long-term process that begins now and won't be complete until our children leave home.

Dear Heavenly Father, I want to have children who behave well, but I am not sure where to start. I have spent all of my baby's life so far giving her everything she wants and needs, always trying to please her. It is so hard to tell her no and see her cry, even when I know that is what is best for her. Help me lovingly begin planting good seeds, gently teaching and training her in right behavior so when she is older, she will live a life pleasing to You. Amen.

Week 47

Day 323

Get out the blocks and have fun building things with your baby. Help her learn to stack two blocks, then three. It will take a steady hand and good coordination for her to be successful. If it is too difficult for her, stack the blocks for her and let her try later.

Day 324

Let your baby experience cause and effect. Hold your baby and help him turn the light switch on and off. He will begin to realize that he is the one causing the light to change. Use the words "on" and "off" as he does it. As you go about your day, let him turn light switches on and off for you when it is convenient.

Day 325

Sing "The Wheels on the Bus" with your baby.

The wheels on the bus   *(move hands in a circle)*
go round and round

Round and round,   *(move hands in a circle)*
round and round

The wheels on the bus go round and round	*(move hands in a circle)*
All through the town	*(lift hands up and out to the sides)*
1. The driver on the bus says, "Move on back"	*(point thumb over shoulder)*
2. The wipers on the bus go swish, swish, swish	*(move arms back and forth)*
3. The horn on the bus goes beep, beep, beep	*(pretend to beep a horn)*

Day 326

Help your baby learn animal sounds. Often they are easier to say than the name for the animal. Tell your baby the sound the animal makes whenever he sees a real one, a picture of one, or a toy one. Use animation in your voice as you say, "The doggy goes woof, woof," or "The cow goes: moo."

Day 327

Blow soap bubbles with your baby. She will enjoy watching them float away or reaching out to touch one. Playing with bubbles makes for some great photographs of her little face as she looks up in awe, smiles with glee, or looks surprised as they pop in her hands. Have your camera ready!

Day 328

Let your baby draw his first picture with crayons. Tape the paper to his high chair tray to keep the paper from moving around. Hand him one crayon at a time. Guide his hand to produce scribbles. Monitor him to make sure he doesn't eat the crayons. Save his masterpiece—the first of many! Label the back with his age.

Day 329

Turn on some music and let your baby wiggle and dance to it. Try all different kinds of music. Dance, sway, march, bounce, and clap to the beat. Let her "feel" the music.

Reflections on the Week

If any of you lacks wisdom, he should ask God, who gives generously to all without finding fault, and it will be given to him.

JAMES 1:5

By wisdom a house is built, and through understanding it is established; through

*knowledge its rooms are filled with rare
and beautiful treasures.*

Proverbs 24:3-4

Learning to Be a Better Mom

Do you think of your position as a mother as a profession, as a calling? It is, and you should give to it as much energy and commitment as you would to any other career. Whether you are still in the workforce or have left it to raise your children, you probably worked hard to excel in your position, continually improving your skills to be more productive. You may have read trade magazines, gone to seminars, taken classes, and networked with others in your field. You need to bring these same skills, creativity, and energy to your job as a mother. Seek out education to become the best mother you can be.

The first place to go for wisdom in your parenting is the Bible. God has plenty to say on how you should live your life and train your children. One place to start would be the book of Proverbs. It is a practical book that gives instruction on godly living. God's Word is the filter through which you should evaluate all other parenting information. As you pursue your parenting education, compare what you learn with what's said in the Bible to make sure the advice doesn't contradict God's Word. There are many parenting philosophies being taught, so be wise in whose counsel you follow.

You can also learn from parenting books and magazines. Listen to Christian radio programs that address parenting issues such as *Focus on the Family* and *Family Life*. Be a student of motherhood by "networking" with your mom friends. Often I get ideas and inspiration to be a better parent by just observing other moms in action. Different moms bring different gifts to their mothering. One might remind me to enjoy my kids as I watch her having a great time playing at the park with her children. Another handles trials and frustrations with a sense of humor, while another can teach me how she has managed to keep her home so well organized. Watching a mother proactively work on her child's character development or show respect to her children by looking at them in the eyes when she speaks to them motivates me to do the same. Another encourages me to be more prayerful as I watch her lift all her concerns up to God in prayer.

We can learn much from other mothers, especially those who have children older than ours. It is helpful to have a role model, someone who has walked the path of motherhood before us. It may be a family member, neighbor, or friend from church who can serve as a mentor. We can learn from her past experience if we have a teachable spirit. She can also objectively look at our situation and help give us a balanced perspective and helpful advice.

*D*ear Lord, there is so much to learn about being a good mother—it looked so easy before I had a child!

Help me to be a good student of motherhood and put as much effort into this career as I have done in my other positions. God, You are the source of all wisdom, and I pray that You would fill me with that wisdom. Help me have a teachable spirit to learn from others. Please place some experienced mothers in my life who can help me in my journey of motherhood. Amen.

Week 48

Day 330

Your baby can use a riding toy now. Make sure the base has a wide support and a low seat. Show her how to sit on the seat with her legs straddled to maintain her balance. Practice inside first on the carpet before you venture outside. It will take some practice before she figures out how to move it. She will probably move backwards first.

Day 331

Your baby is learning how to let go of and drop things. This is an exciting new skill for him as his fingers gain more dexterity. Show him how to drop small blocks into a box one at a time. Let him take the blocks out and try it on his own. He will love to fill and empty the box. Stress the words "in" and "out" as he does this.

Day 332

Take your baby to the local pond and let her watch you feed the ducks. They will put on quite a show for her. She will get to hear the ducks say, "Quack, quack."

Day 333

Set up an obstacle course for your baby to go through. Put out things for him to crawl over, under, and around. You could use pillows, beach balls, boxes, and chairs.

Day 334

It will be awhile before your baby knows his colors, but begin now to point them out. Say, "Let's wear our red shirt," or "Look at the pretty pink flower," or "You have on blue pants like Mommy has on blue pants."

Your Baby Is Eleven Months Old!

Day 335

Glue a photograph of each family member onto the sides of a small tissue box. Cover the photos with clear adhesive paper to protect them. Show the pictures to your baby and talk about who they are. Give the box to him and say, "Where's Daddy's picture?" Praise him when he finds it. Do the same for the other pictures.

Day 336

Hold both of your baby's hands so she can practice walking. It will probably be several months before she is walking on her own, but she will enjoy practicing with your assistance. Bare floors can often be cold on little feet, but socks are dangerously slippery. Make your own nonskid socks by applying dots of fabric puff paint to the soles of her socks.

Reflections on the Week

Never be lacking in zeal, but keep your spiritual fervor, serving the Lord. Be joyful in hope, patient in affliction, faithful in prayer.

ROMANS 12:11-12

Trust in the LORD with all your heart and lean not on your own understanding; in all your ways acknowledge him, and he will make your paths straight.

PROVERBS 3:5-6

Grow in Your Relationship with the Lord

Motherhood will keep you busy, but be careful not to completely neglect your spiritual life. Now that your baby is able to entertain herself for longer periods, carve out some time to spend with God each day in prayer and reading His Word. He longs for you to spend time with Him. Just as your baby needs milk to grow, you need God's Word to deepen your faith.

The spiritual side of our lives colors everything we do, yet it is often neglected. As mothers we have a responsibility to become spiritually mature, because we can't model or teach what we don't know. We have to begin with ourselves. We need to nurture our relationship with God and grow in our faith if we want to raise godly children. It is only through God's power that we can become the calm, peaceful, gentle, loving mothers we want to be. We need to allow Him to change our hearts so we are able to respond to our children in a more Christlike manner.

Find a time of day that works—first thing in the morning, naptime, or before you go to bed—and try to spend at least ten uninterrupted minutes reading the Bible and praying. Focus on being in God's presence. You can go through a book of the Bible or study what God has to say on a specific topic by using a concordance. As you saturate your mind with His Word, your thoughts, actions, and attitude will become more like His. You will come away refreshed and replenished for your family.

Dear God, I get so busy planning and running my life that I neglect to spend time with You. Please forgive me. Help me to set my priorities better. Thank You that You are always available to me. I long to deepen my relationship with You and spend more time in Your presence. Help me to become more like You as I spend time in Your Word and in prayer. Amen.

Week 49

Day 337

Tell your baby today how precious she is to both you and to God. Tell her all the wonderful things that you love about her. Even though she can't understand all your words, she will know what you are feeling by the tone of your voice and your gentle touch.

Day 338

Help your baby become aware of the parts of his face. Point to and name your baby's facial features, your own, a stuffed animal's, or those of a face in a magazine. As he begins learning the names of his body parts, it's helpful to reintroduce some of the songs you sang earlier in the year. Putting things to music helps us learn more quickly. Try "Head, Shoulders, Knees and Toes," "The Hokey Pokey," and "If You're Happy and You Know It."

Day 339

Go for a walk and show your baby some flowers. Talk about how God made so many different, beautiful flowers to decorate the world. Show her how to smell the flowers (she will probably blow rather than sniff at first).

Day 340

Sing this silly song with your baby.

Bah - rump went the little green frog one day	*(squat and jump)*
Bah - rump went the little green frog	*(squat and jump)*
Bah - rump went the little green frog one day	*(squat and jump)*
And her eyes went blink, blink, blink	*(blink your eyes)*

Day 341

Let your baby learn different words by experiencing them. Show her what the opposite of the word means to help place the word in context. Do these activities throughout the day while saying the word.

- Lift your baby "up" then "down."
- Give her a "full" cup then an "empty" cup.
- Touch something "hot" then "cold."
- Wash "dirty" hands to make them "clean."
- Roll a "big" ball then a "little" ball.
- Touch a "wet" towel then a "dry" one.
- Turn a light "on" then "off."
- Make a "sad" face then a "happy" face.

Day 342

Sit your baby in the middle of a large sheet. Next, you and your husband should each hold two corners and shake the sheet to make waves (be gentle at first). Your baby will enjoy seeing the sheet move all around her and feeling the breeze. As long as you have the sheet out, put it over the back of a couple chairs and make a tent for all of you to crawl into.

Day 343

During those difficult moments and tiring days, always remember what a gift and blessing your child is. Don't allow the frustrations and difficulties you encounter to blot out the joy your precious child can bring. If you need to refocus on the positive, try writing down ten things you love about your baby or ten things that did go right today.

Reflections on the Week

Finally, all of you, live in harmony with one another; be sympathetic, love as brothers, be compassionate and humble. Do not repay evil with evil or insult with insult, but with blessing, because to this you were called so that you may inherit a blessing.

1 Peter 3:8-9

Whoever loves his brother lives in the light, and there is nothing in him to make him stumble.

1 John 2:10

Brothers and Sisters

Maybe you have older children or are thinking about having another child. Watching a friendship bloom between siblings can be one of the greatest joys of parenting, but it doesn't usually just happen. You have to help them learn to get along, be friends, and manage conflict. It will take work on your part.

Siblings help children learn to realize that they are not the center of the universe. They learn to wait, share, think of other's needs before their own, and respect others and their differences. In return, they get a lifelong friend who knows them better than anyone else.

Begin by instilling in them that God has placed them together in a family. He handpicked who your children's siblings would be, and He chose the very best ones for them. Your family is a team; God put you together for a purpose. Encourage a loving relationship between your children. They must be taught to be kind and respectful to each other, just as they would treat a friend. Never allow your children to hurt each other physically or verbally. Don't allow name-calling or put-downs. They can learn to treat each other with respect even when they don't agree. Don't just let your children battle it out. Young children do not intuitively know how to work out their differences in a socially acceptable way. They need to be trained and given tools in how to manage conflict and resolve problems. This is a process, but if you start from the beginning, you can circumvent many problems in the future.

When you become pregnant or are in the process of adoption, start planting the seeds. Tell your child, "I know you are going to be such a good big brother." After your baby arrives, give your older child a vision for the future by saying, "One day he is going to be your best friend," or "Our baby is so lucky to have you as a big brother," or "Look how you make him laugh. He really likes you!" When you are doing something with your older child tell your baby, "You are going to have to wait for a minute while I finish helping your big brother." Your baby won't understand, but your older child will appreciate knowing he is not the only one who has to wait.

Give them breaks from each other. You would have a hard time getting along with someone every waking moment too. Separate them before sparks begin to fly; don't wait until there is a major dispute. Be proactive. Teach and enforce the Golden Rule—"Do to others as you would have them do to you" (Luke 6:31).

*D*ear Lord, thank You for this family You have given me. Please be at work in all of us so we can become a close-knit family. Please help me cultivate my children's friendship. Let us be a family that loves and respects each other and enjoys each other's company. Amen.

Week 50

Day 344

Teach your child to come to you when you call. This could save his life one day. When he is crawling, tell him, "Come to Mommy." When he comes to you, praise him by saying, "Good boy, _____. You obeyed Mommy!" and give him a big hug. Play a game with your baby and your husband. Sit a short distance across from each other with your baby on your lap. Your husband says, "Come to Daddy." Let him crawl over to Daddy for a big hug. Now you say, "Come to Mommy," and your baby will crawl back to you. Let it be a fun game while he learns to respond to your words.

Day 345

Save an empty plastic jar with a screw-on lid (popcorn and peanut butter are often in these kinds of jars). Screw the lid on very lightly and then show your baby how to turn the lid to unscrew it. Put some toys in the jar to motivate her to take off the lid. This will help develop her fine motor skills.

Day 346

When you give your baby directions, break them into simple steps. It will be awhile before she can follow two-part directions. Say, "Get the ball" and then wait until she gets the ball. Then say, "Throw the ball to Mommy." This shouldn't be a drill, but rather integrated into your day as you play with her.

Day 347

Hold up your baby's hand. Start with the pinkie finger as you touch each fingertip. Say "Johnny" (or your baby's name) as you touch each one. When you get to his pointer finger, slide your finger down his pointer finger and up the thumb saying "Whoops." Touch the thumb and say "Johnny," then slide your finger back down his thumb and up his pointer finger, saying "Whoops" again. Then touch each of the fingertips back to the pinkie saying "Johnny" as you touch them.

Day 348

Get an empty banana box from the produce department of your grocery store. Cut a few small holes on the side if there are not some already (just in case she puts it over her head). Let your baby push it around, giving her favorite stuffed animal a ride. She can sit in it and pretend it is a boat, an airplane, a car, or a train. Give her a ride and push her in the box.

Day 349

The next time it rains, bring your baby outside for a moment to let him see, feel, listen, taste, and smell the rain. Bring him back inside and let him watch the raindrops roll down the window. Sing:

> *The rain is falling down—splash*
> *The rain is falling down*
> *Pitter, patter*
> *Pitter, patter*
> *Rain is falling down—splash!*

Day 350

Get a wooden puzzle with little knobs on the pieces. Let your baby take the pieces out of the frame. Name the objects on the puzzle pieces. It will be awhile before she can put the pieces back in herself, so help her with it. Let her take the pieces out again.

Reflections on the Week

> *No discipline seems pleasant at the time,*
> *but painful. Later on, however, it produces*
> *a harvest of righteousness and peace for*
> *those who have been trained by it.*

HEBREWS 12:11

Children, obey your parents in the Lord, for this is right. Fathers, do not exasperate your children; instead, bring them up in the training and instruction of the Lord.

EPHESIANS 6:1,4

How to Discipline Your Child

As your baby becomes more mobile, you need to constantly keep an eye on her. She will find plenty of opportunities to get herself into trouble. She is also beginning to assert her own will, believing she is in charge and should be able to do whatever she wants. Your responsibility to train and discipline your child really comes into play now. When you teach and train your child early, you are ingraining patterns of right behavior. It is much more difficult to correct bad behavior that has been allowed to become a habit than if you deal with it immediately.

Make sure your child doesn't have too many "no's" in her day. Life for her and for you won't be very pleasant if you are always reprimanding. She should have plenty of opportunities to explore and investigate the world around her. On the other hand, you are doing her no favor by allowing her to do whatever she pleases. One of the first areas where your child learns the meaning of no and how to use self-control is in not touching things that are off limits to her. It is not necessary to remove everything in your house that you don't want her to touch (of course, anything dangerous or valuable should be removed). Don't be surprised when she tests you to find out just how firm those limits are. Be consistent in correcting the behaviors and actions that you have decided are unacceptable.

When you discipline your children, you should be proactive. Look for teachable moments in everyday situations to help them better understand your expectations. Show them the right way to do things, instead of just reprimanding them when they do something wrong. You can't expect them to instinctively know what you expect of them. Discipline isn't just about correcting wrong behavior; you must also praise good behavior. Look for times when your children are doing something right, and then shower them with hugs, kisses, and words of praise.

The goal in disciplining is to teach, not punish. Try to have realistic expectations for their behavior and to be respectful in how you treat them—remember righteous behavior is a process in which we, as adults, are still being refined. Never discipline out of anger or frustration, but instead do it with love and kindness. It is possible to be kind and yet firm at the same time. Always communicate by your words and actions that, though you are not happy with their behavior, there is nothing your children could ever do that will change your love for them.

Dear Lord, I am so thankful You are present in my life because I feel so ill-equipped in some parts of my job as a mother. Lord, give me wisdom and discernment in

knowing when and how to begin disciplining my child. Help me to not discipline out of anger, frustration, or weariness. Let my child always sense my love for her. Please help me be patient, consistent, and loving as I raise this child, so one day her life will glorify You. Amen.

Week 51

Day 351

Let your baby try eating with a spoon. Custard-style yogurt is a good food to start with because it tends to stay on the spoon better. Hold the container and help her dip the spoon into the yogurt. Help guide the spoon into her mouth. Now let her try by herself, helping as needed and holding the container. When she becomes more interested in dipping her hand into the container or flinging the yogurt off the spoon than eating, take the yogurt away as she probably isn't hungry anymore. Self-feeding will be messy at first and will provide you with some cute photo opportunities, but you don't want to let it get out of control. Remember, train her in good habits from the beginning so you won't have to retrain her later.

Day 352

Take a quick succession of photos when your baby learns to walk. These pictures will be priceless. The first could be of him holding onto something for support. The next one would be of him letting go. The next could be of him taking that first tentative step. The final shot could be the look of pride and excitement on his face as he reaches his destination point. Mat four of these pictures in sequential order so you can always remember his first steps.

Day 353

Sing and act out the words to this song with your baby.

Teddy bear, teddy   *(turn around)*
bear, turn around

Teddy bear, teddy   *(touch the ground)*
bear, touch the ground

Teddy bear, teddy   *(point your shoe out)*
bear, show your shoe

Teddy bear, teddy   *(sit down)*
bear, that will do.

Day 354

Point to your nose and your baby's nose. Say, "God gave us a nose so we can breathe and smell." Amazingly, your baby has been able to recognize your scent from his very first days. Let him experience many different smells by going on an olfactory tour of your house. Let him smell different things like vanilla, soap, cinnamon, perfume, shampoo, flowers, and scented candles.

Day 355

Place some Play-Doh on your baby's high chair tray. Shape it into a thick pancake. Help him poke holes in the Play-Doh with his finger. Give him the handle of a wooden spoon to poke more holes. Let him squish it in his hands. He will love playing with the dough, but make sure he doesn't start eating it since usually whatever is put on his tray is for him to eat.

Day 356

Go for a walk with your baby. Bring a bag or bucket. Let her collect treasures—rocks, twigs, leaves, and dandelions. When you get home, dump out her treasures and let her hold them while you talk about them with her (be careful she doesn't put them in her mouth).

Day 357

At the dinner table say, "Where's Mommy?" or "Where's Daddy?" or anyone else in your family. Let her point to the correct person. She may just look at the correct person, but you can point and say, "Yes, there's Mommy!"

Reflections on the Week

For the Lord grants wisdom!...He shows how to distinguish right from wrong, how to find the right decision every time. For wisdom and truth will enter the very

*center of your being, filling your life with
joy.*

PROVERBS 2:6,9-10 TLB

*Be very careful, then, how you live—not
as unwise but as wise.*

EPHESIANS 5:15

Use Your Time Wisely

During this busy season of life, we often need to be
reminded to use our time wisely. We have to evaluate how
much time we can commit to outside activities before it
has a negative effect on our parenting. This is a difficult
decision because most of our activities and commitments
are probably good ones. They might include volunteer
work, an outside job, a ministry at church, redecorating
our home, or a time-consuming hobby or sport. We need
to ask ourselves, do these commitments take us away from
using our energy and skills on what is really important—
raising our children? Are we giving our families our best or
just the leftovers because we have already given our best
to others? Even when we are physically present with our
children, our minds may be a million miles away, preoccupied, thinking about other responsibilities. Our schedules
should reflect our priorities.

This is a difficult balancing act, but you can go to God
in prayer for wisdom and discernment in when to say yes
and when to say no. You don't have to say no to everything.
God may want you to say yes to some things. Be realistic
about how much you can handle, which is not necessarily

what your friends, church members, or society think you can handle. I have a friend who had a great revelation one day when she realized that just because someone thought she would be good at something and asked her to do it, did not necessarily mean it was God's will for her!

Before you say yes, know what you are committing to. You are undoubtedly very talented, which is why you are given so many opportunities to work, serve, and minister, but those talents won't fade away. In fact, you can use these very same skills, talents, and wisdom to bless your family. You will have plenty of time in the future to share them with others. Your family is your first priority. When you start juggling fewer plates, you can stop rushing and slow down. You will be more relaxed with your children and more in tune with their needs. You will have more time to be the kind of mother you want to be.

Dear Lord, there are so many things I want to do, feel I should do, or am asked to do. They are all good, important things, but perhaps they are not the best things to be doing when I am the mother of a young baby. Please give me wisdom, discernment, and even the courage to know when to say no. Help me use my time and energy in ways that will bring glory and honor to You. Amen.

Week 52

Day 358

Go in and gaze at your baby while he sleeps. Admire his peaceful face and tousled hair. Look at how much he has grown and yet is still such a little baby. Enjoy these peaceful, reflective moments while he is "charging up his batteries" for another active day tomorrow.

Day 359

Play "Ring Around the Rosey." Your baby will be able to practice her steps and will enjoy anticipating the surprise and excitement of falling down.

Day 360

Even though your baby can't say much yet, he understands quite a bit. To find out how much he understands, set a ball and a spoon in front of him. Point to and name both objects. Ask him where the ball is. See if he picks up the ball. If he doesn't, help him choose correctly. Do the same with the spoon. Try using different objects. This game will also help him learn to listen and follow directions.

Day 361

When you look at a book together, ask her where something is on the page. Let her point to the correct picture. If she needs help, guide her hand to point to it.

Day 362

Do this finger play with your baby.

Clap, clap, clap your hands as slowly as you can   (clap and talk slowly)

Clap, clap, clap your hands as quickly as you can   (clap and talk quickly)

1. Roll, roll, roll your hands...

2. Wiggle, wiggle, wiggle your fingers...

3. Pound, pound, pound your fist...

Day 363

Keep a birthday book for your child using a blank journal. Each year on his birthday, write him a love letter telling him why he is so special. Write about his accomplishments and any special memories from the past year. Tell him about your hopes and dreams for him and how much you love him. It will be a treasured keepsake for your child in the years to come! You may even want to photocopy the letter and put it in a safe deposit box.

Day 364

Videotape your baby's first birthday. Make sure you get her eating her cake (this is one time you should let her eat with reckless abandon!). Record the filming on a special birthday video. Each year add new birthday party footage. It will be fun to watch each year to see how much your child has grown and how her personality has blossomed. If you have some video of her on the day she was born, you may want to put this on the beginning of the tape.

Day 365

Congratulations! You made it through the first year of your baby's life! You have watched him or her grow and change so quickly. Part of you may want to keep your child a baby forever, while the other part of you looks forward to all the excitement yet to come. The time you have spent with your baby has built a solid foundation of love and trust between the two of you. These are the most important gifts you could ever give your precious child. Well done!

Your Baby Is One Year Old!

Reflections on the Week

I tell you the truth, unless you change and become like little children, you will never enter the kingdom of heaven. Therefore, whoever humbles himself like this child is the greatest in the kingdom of heaven. And whoever welcomes a little child like this in my name welcomes me.

MATTHEW 18:3-5

And we, who with unveiled faces all reflect the Lord's glory, are being transformed into his likeness with ever-increasing glory, which comes from the Lord.

2 CORINTHIANS 3:18

Our Children Change Us for the Better

Are you beginning to feel like a different person from how you were before you had children? Motherhood will transform you. It is a crash course in selflessness. It can, however, be a slow, difficult process. There are days you might not even recognize yourself, especially if you always prided yourself on being patient, kind, and in control. Who is this woman who has such an impressive resumé of accomplishments and yet can't even keep up with the laundry, this woman who could be patient with the most difficult client and is now so impatient with a helpless, crying baby? Slowly over time, however, we begin to see God at work in us.

Motherhood stretches us, humbles us, and forces us to grow up and become better people. We are slowly becoming more loving, caring, selfless, compassionate, patient, tender, thoughtful, and kind. We have learned to focus on someone other than ourselves.

We begin to amaze ourselves with the number of tasks we can complete at one time. Motherhood increases our talents and skills. God uses our children to mold us into the women He wants us to be.

You will probably find yourself looking at the world differently now. Everything is new, wonderful, and fascinating. Bugs and fire engines and sparkly rocks may be things you never noticed before. Motherhood adds an extra dimension to who you are, uncovering parts of you that may have been long forgotten. You learn to be more silly, carefree, and uninhibited. Your baby brings out the many sides of you that others don't see. You are a far richer person now that you are a mother!

Dear Heavenly Father, thank You for helping me to become a better person through my baby. I love him so much that I would do anything for him. Some days I can love and care for him so selflessly, and other days I feel so selfish. Help transform me into the woman You want me to be. Give me new eyes to see and enjoy the world as my baby does. Thank You for this sweet child and all the things he has taught me. I have loved spending this first year with him, and I can't wait to see what's in store for us next! Amen.

May the Lord Bless You

Your little baby has turned one year old! The time has passed by so quickly, yet there is much to look forward to in the years ahead. I feel very blessed to have been able to share a part of your baby's first year with you!

This is my prayer for you and your baby as you continue on this exciting journey of motherhood:

May the Lord richly bless and protect
both you and your children.

May the Lord's face radiate with joy
because of you;

May he be gracious to you,
show you his favor,
and give you his peace.

Amen.

PSALM 115:14 AND NUMBERS 6:24-26 TLB

Other Harvest House Reading

The Power of a Praying® Parent
Stormie Omartian

The first book in Stormie Omartian's bestselling The Power of a Praying® series guides parents in 30 simple chapters to effectively pray for their children's safety, faith, purity, and character. Become the praying parent you want to be.

Prayers for My Baby Girl/Prayers for My Baby Boy
Angela Thomas

Bestselling author Angela Thomas is an adoring mom whose prayers, presented as letters to God, celebrate delight in the wonder of a newborn boy or girl. These tender tributes to new life and the divine gift of motherhood are bundled with Julie Johnson's captivating, heartwarming photos of sweet babies.

For This Child I Prayed
Stormie Omartian

Anyone dedicated to supporting a child in infancy and beyond will thrill to the cherished prayers, Scriptures, and insights Stormie offers. This lovely keepsake features Susan Rios' tender paintings of children in their formative years.